Why Lean Transformation Fails

Why Lean Transformation Fails

Overcoming Challenges to Adopting New
Leadership and Management Systems

Editor and Contributor Steven Leuschel
Foreword by Bob Emiliani

Align Kaizen Publishing
Indiana, Pennsylvania

© 2019 by Align Kaizen Publishing

Published by
Align Kaizen Publishing
Indiana, PA 15701

Printed in the United States of America.

ISBN-13: 978-0-9991897-3-3

A special thanks to the authors, publishers, and copyright holders for permission to reproduce material.

Cataloging-in-Publication (CIP) data—see http://loc.gov/publish/cip/

Table of Contents

WARNING: The word "fail" may aggravate mental allergies for some. Please refer to the definition:

Fail

verb

\ ˈfāl \

failed; **failing**; **fails**
Definition of *fail*
intransitive verb
1a: to lose strength : WEAKEN
~~**b:** to fade or die away~~
~~**c:** to stop functioning normally~~
2a: to fall short
b: to be or become ~~absent or~~ inadequate
~~**c:** to be unsuccessful~~
~~**d:** to become bankrupt or insolvent~~

transitive verb

1a: to disappoint the expectations or trust of
b: to miss performing an expected service or function for
~~**2:** to be deficient in : LACK~~
~~**3:** to leave undone : NEGLECT~~
~~**4a:** to be unsuccessful in passing~~
~~**b:** to grade (someone, such as a student) as not passing~~

Mariam-Webster Dictionary, 2019

Foreword

The change from the current way of managing an organization, classical management, to the future way of managing an organization, Lean management, is a process. In the more than 30 years since Lean became known to the public, the transformation process has remained poorly defined and seen as dependent on each organization's unique circumstances. For this and other reasons, all organizations who attempt a Lean transformation struggle and most fail – where failure is defined as neither achieving the necessary changes in a leadership team's beliefs, behaviors, and competencies, nor the physical changes necessary to achieve material and information flow. In other words, failure means the inability to transform both the social and technical expressions of management practice. This typically culminates in the abandonment of the pursuit of Lean as a new system of management. As James P. Womack recently said: "We have not seen the scale or magnitude of lean transformations we hoped to see.[1]"

After all these years, why hasn't Lean transformation been codified into a standardized, repeatable process, perhaps something like open-source software, where the process (code) is continuously improved by qualified parties? We have several well-documented examples of organizations that have successfully transformed, from which we can easily recognize the similar paths that they followed. Is it necessary to produce a detailed, stepwise process from these successful examples for others to follow, or will a basic framework provide the needed guidance? If one develops such a detailed stepwise process, will an organization's top leaders follow it? And, most importantly, will the top leaders be part of the transformation process as they all were in our most successful examples? Over the decades, we have learned that most leaders do not want to be part of the transformation process, so they delegate it to people inside the organization, to consultants, or both. When this happens, a standardized transformation process is made useless because senior leaders, who are key participants, purposefully withhold their participation.

The lack of leadership engagement to learn Lean management and undergo the needed changes in leadership beliefs, behaviors, and competencies is one clearly identifiable mode by which the Lean transformation process fails. But there is another mode by which the process fails. When the threshold is finally crossed and Lean transformation is achieved, it faces a very high risk of being undone – reverting to classical management – due to changes in leadership or changes in company ownership. Because such changes are inevitable, Lean transformation is often ephemeral. It takes ongoing vigilance and special preparations to ensure that classical management, in whole or part, does not re-emerge in an organization. The failure of Lean transformation processes and its undoing by new leaders or owners are the two most pressing problems of our time.

The idea of "Lean failure" is controversial. If one attaches the word "failure" to "Lean," then a perception may be formed that Lean transformation is difficult and should be avoided. This, of course, could unfavorably affect the interests of those who promote Lean management. Some people strongly argue that "Lean failure" does not exist; that there is no such thing as failure in pursuit of Lean transformation. They say this with the maximum of confidence, but it is a mistake to equate confidence with competence, as this leads people into being fooled.

More specifically, they say that trying hard in one's practice of Lean management is indicative of success, even if little improvement has been achieved in fundamental business performance: productivity improvement, cost reduction, shorter lead times, higher quality, safety improvements, and so on. Effort matters more than the results achieved. This is true, but only up to a point, as failure is part of the learning process—i.e., as what not to do again and as inspiration for new ideas to try. Others say "Lean [itself] can't fail, only people fail." One vocal critic argues that "Lean can't fail just like English can't fail." What can fail, of course, is the process of writing in the English language, resulting in bad prose that is easily recognized as having failed to achieve its goal of effective communication. As I have emphasized in previous passages, Lean transformation is a process, and the inability to achieve stated or desired business goals enabled by Lean transformation represents failure. After much study, we now know that Lean transformation is difficult due to a network of interconnected causes that are intrinsic to the institution of leadership.

Anyone who tackles this sensitive subject immediately earns a badge of distinction for bravery and courage. It is a subject that most people prefer to ignore. But how can improvement in Lean transformation processes be achieved if problems are ignored? One must recognize the problems, acknowledge the facts as they exist, generate ideas, and make improvements so that others may succeed. One must think critically and apply the Plan-Do-Check-Act (PDCA) cycle to the Lean transformation process. Unfortunately, it has been the routine since the emergence of Lean over thirty years ago for its advocates to focus on success stories and largely ignore people's struggles and the failed Lean transformations. They somehow believe there is nothing to learn from failure, when, in fact, there is more to learn from failure than there is to learn from success.

The proof that "Lean failure" exists is in the recent shift away from emphasizing the need for organizations to achieve a Lean transformation. The new emphasis by Lean community leaders is the skilled application of Lean methods and tools for solving day-to-day problems. This shift makes sense, as there has never been much demand from CEOs for Lean transformation. What CEOs want is employees who are better problem-solvers. They want employees who are highly skilled at using various problem-solving processes—Lean or otherwise—and at driving to understand and correct the root causes of problems in the workplace.

Despite this emerging change in focus, there remains a pressing need to better understand the nature and causes of Lean transformation process failure. People work hard to understand and apply Lean principles, methods, and tools. They and their efforts are respected when we carefully and critically inquire into the causes of their struggles. Lean transformation process failure must be examined scientifically, rather than anecdotally as has been the case in the past. This is important because Lean transformation remains a desirable goal, and there will always be interest in Lean transformation by both leaders and followers. In addition, there could come a day when businesses are forced by circumstances to transform to Lean management. Therefore, our job is to think scientifically, discover the facts, and propose improvements to Lean transformation processes. We must learn from the mistakes of others as well as through our own mistakes. This is how new knowledge and know-how are generated, evolved, and passed on from one generation to the next.

In recent years, a growing number of academics and practitioners have begun to study the causes of Lean transformation failure. *Why Lean Transformation Fails* is an important addition to this body of literature. A clear picture of cause-and-effect is now emerging, which allows meaningful corrective action to be taken. Steven Leuschel has organized and synthesized diverse information that delivers a consensus view of the top-level factors that lead to Lean transformation process success and failure. He has done great work in sorting through the clutter and confusion and presents a concise and impactful distillation to readers.

Each chapter is short but robust in content and is perfectly fitted to executive's limited time and attention bandwidth. The information contained in the book is entirely practical and each chapter finishes with a "Things to Consider" table that provides a short but extremely useful listing of dos and don'ts. The book concludes with a summary of the reasons why all Lean transformation processes struggle and why most fail, followed by a "Lean Challenge Assessment" that can be used in several different ways.

Why Lean Transformation Fails shines a bright light on an important problem that too many people have preferred to ignore. Overall, readers will find the book to be a very helpful guide at any point of an organization's Lean transformation process. Knowing this information will help improve Lean transformation processes which, in turn, could revitalize interest in Lean transformation. In addition, I expect this and related works to contribute to making Lean management itself ever-better as they simultaneously expand our understanding of Lean leadership.

Finally, I congratulate readers for taking an interest in this problem and seeking to learn more about it. From new knowledge comes new ideas to try, which leads to the development of new capabilities and wisdom for creating a better tomorrow for employees, business, and society.

Professor Bob Emiliani

April 2019
South Kingstown, Rhode Island
www.bobemiliani.com

Notes

1. J.P. Womack, "James P. Womack Scholarship & Philanthropy Fund," https://www.lean.org/jpwfund, Lean Enterprise Institute, accessed 2 April 2019

For a detailed analysis of the institution of leadership and how it reacts to new ideas and change, see the book *The Triumph of Classical Management Over Lean Management: How Tradition Prevails and What to Do About It* by Bob Emiliani, 2018.

Preface

Why Lean Transformation Fails is a compilation of original and republished content from both researchers and practitioners. This book is for senior leaders and those architecting transformations to study when initiating or reinvigorating a Lean journey. *Why Lean Transformation Fails* is brief to give folks with limited time a conversation piece for learning common barriers, diagnosing initiatives, and creating more proactive Lean transformation plans.

The purpose of *Why Lean Transformation Fails* is to present both common challenges and historical barriers to Lean, Operational Excellence, and other Toyota Production System (TPS)-like techniques. Problems are blessings—opportunities to improve—so the problems and barriers in this book are not meant as negatives but rather opportunities for other organizations and leaders to learn and improve.

Unfortunately, though, the thought that Lean transformations can actually fail carries a stigma of negativity that many Lean practitioners and Lean thought leaders want to ignore, look beyond, or dismiss. This book isn't meant to be negative—it's meant to be real: if your organization attempts Lean transformation you will most likely encounter many of the barriers and failure modes I have outlined in this book. In the best cases, leaders can proactively avoid failure modes. But, in other cases, just acknowledging these failure modes when they occur is the first step in problem-solving.

Grasping common causes of transformation failures helps perpetuate mutual trust and respect. Additionally, rather than self-diagnosing using internal anecdotes that may focus on or blame a particular person, this book allows leaders to learn from other organizations' mistakes to keep discussions positive and proactive within their organization.

I chose to compile this book because many organizations have been and continue to be inspired by Toyota and have tried to become "Lean." Many, if not all have failed at some point either temporarily or permanently. Merriam-Webster's 2019 definition of fail can be summed up as: to lose strength; to fall short; to become inadequate; to not meet expectations; or to miss achieving an expected target. Please note that failures are not necessarily permanent and create opportunities to improve. However, ignoring opportunities to improve and not learning from them may cause permanent failure and abandonment of Lean transformation techniques.

I hope that *Why Lean Transformation Fails* will educate both practitioners and executives on the pitfalls and barriers associated with adapting the TPS-like techniques to advance mutual trust, respect, and prosperity.

Introduction

In 2005, I was introduced to adaptations of the Toyota Production System, which we called Operational Excellence, learning from Rodger Lewis, a former Toyota leader, and David Adams, the Executive Director at Saint Vincent College's Kennametal Center for Operational Excellence. Our focus was coaching an *organizational transformation process*. Yes, every organization is different, but in our experiences organizations generally go through these high-level steps:

1. Grasping the business case
2. Engaging senior leadership
3. Continuous improvement training / implementation
4. Establishing a pilot area
5. Stabilizing and extending the transformation
6. Sustaining the transformation

Like any other process, each of these process steps has failure modes. Therefore, this book follows the same overall process steps with slight modifications to identify Lean transformation challenges in the order that they may likely occur:

Imperatives of Lean Transformation

Chapter 1 contains a republished article by Virginia Mason Medical Center's Gary Kaplan and others. Virginia Mason is a highly regarded Lean healthcare organization and Dr. Kaplan et al. wrote *Why Lean Doesn't Work for Everyone*. Additionally, I discuss Lean challenges with leadership, management systems, and culture.

Starting Lean Transformation

In Chapter 2, I expand upon my work in an appendix of *Lean Culture Change* and discuss why many organizations may have started Lean as well as the challenges associated with starting Lean. For this chapter, I use the theory of the Iron Cage by DiMaggio and Powell to help explain this phenomenon of organizations becoming more similar. Additionally, an article repeatedly cited is Phillip Marksberry's *Investigating the Way for Toyota Suppliers*, which demonstrates what Toyota requires and does not require of its suppliers. Using that, I explore the potential impact on the diffusion of Lean and failure modes encountered over the last few decades due to Toyota's requirements on its suppliers.

Learning from the Pilot

In Chapter 3, I discuss a few anecdotes on failure modes when transferring Lean concepts to healthcare. Additionally, I use republished content to help explore the challenges of the joint venture with General Motors and Toyota at New United Motor Manufacturing Incorporated (NUMMI). Then I explore how leaders can mitigate similar challenges experienced by General Motors.

Extending Lean Transformation

Chapter 4 discusses challenges with the Saskatchewan Lean Transformation, one of the largest attempts in healthcare to date. Also, this chapter dissects challenges with rolling-out lean production systems using a republished article with subsequent discussion and analysis.

Sustaining Lean Transformation

Chapter 5 discusses the rise and fall of Saturn—which emulated Toyota and General Motor's NUMMI plant in terms of culture and production. Saturn, in my opinion, was GM's first and last chance to essentially create a culture of mutual trust and respect. Unfortunately, it eventually failed when Saturn closed its doors and the brand ceased to exist. This chapter also discusses the end of Wiremold, a Lean implementation model before its buy out. After the buyout, as discussed in this chapter based on Bob Emiliani's book, the culture dramatically changed and Lean transformation ceased.

Finally, Appendix A contains a Lean Challenge Assessment, combining questions and anecdotes found in the book. Keeping track of the Lean Challenge Assessment results on a quarterly or annual basis may give leadership teams anecdotal evidence of the Lean transformation process and further identify Lean transformation failure modes.

These stories, anecdotes, and pieces of advice to avoid failures should demonstrate to readers that Lean transformation challenges not only exist, but they are inevitable. Ignoring the fact that Lean transformations fail will most likely lead to failure. However, Lean practitioners can learn from other organizations' past mistakes and proactively plan for Lean transformation challenges.

I recommend taking notes and re-reading this book at every pivotal moment in the Lean transformation process. Most likely, different challenges may become more evident and need further explored at different times in the transformation process. Understanding why Lean transformation fails doesn't have to be negative. Stay positive by being proactive to the many challenges of Lean transformation.

Enjoy your transformation journey!
-*Steven R. Leuschel*

CHAPTER 1

Lean Transformation Imperatives

The first challenge of Lean transformation occurs before the journey even begins: identifying the imperatives, purpose, and high-level strategies. A leader's connotation of "Lean" may be the first indication of the purpose of starting Lean and may also suggest the challenges ahead for the organization. One study found that Lean was defined in four ways:[1]

- Generic representation of the Toyota Production System
- Process improvement methodology
- Ideological movement that progressed over time
- Polarized body of literature developed over time

Leaders, then, may choose Lean to solve a specific problem, improve processes, or transform an organization. Selecting Lean to solve a problem or improve a process may be a valid use of the Lean tool kit but is not transformational, as discussed by the authors of Article 1, *Why Lean Doesn't Work for Everyone*. This is the opening article for the book because the authors clearly recognize that Lean terminology and tools have permeated healthcare, manufacturing, and other industries while also citing its disappointing results. The authors are a part of Virginia Mason Medical Center, a healthcare system that was one of the first to use Lean and is likely the longest-lasting example in healthcare.

The authors argue that true Lean is *transformational* and not simply implementing traditional Lean tools and doing Lean events. The imperatives of Lean transformation include new management systems, leadership styles, and institutional culture change.

Article 1: "Why Lean Doesn't Work for Everyone"

Gary S. Kaplan, Sarah H. Patterson, Joan M. Ching, C. Craig Blackmore

Introduction

Lean, and other industrial improvement methodologies, are increasingly touted as solutions to the quality and cost challenges in healthcare. However, despite infiltration of Lean terminology into the vernacular of healthcare delivery, and the encroachment of exotic 'Kaizen' quality improvement events into hospital conference rooms, results have often been disappointing.[2]

In the year 2000, Virginia Mason Medical Center in Seattle, Washington, USA, for the first time faced severe financial challenges threatening the continued long-term viability of the institution. Following the quality concerns highlighted by the Institute of Medicine reports on patient safety,[3,4] the organization was shocked in 2004 by the occurrence of an avoidable medical error leading directly to the death of a patient.[5] This stark awareness of quality and cost concerns drove us to explore and subsequently adopt the Lean methodology of the Toyota Production System as our management method.[6] Though our Lean journey is still early when compared to the 60 years of experience at Toyota, once clear lesson has been that the delivery of safer, more efficient, and higher quality, patient-centered care requires not simply the use of Lean tools and events, but rather organizational transformation based on Lean principles. In this report, we summarize what is needed for this arduous journey and explore why Lean doesn't work for everyone.

Transformation at our organization relies on what we term the 'Virginia Mason Production System' (VMPS), our adoption of the Toyota Production System to healthcare. The use of 'Virginia Mason' emphasizes that we have ownership for implementing and improving a methodology that has grown organically at our institution. Implementation at other institutions will cause new eponymous production systems to grow to meet each specific institutional circumstance. We use the term 'Production System' because it is comprehensive, underlying all our work in creating the perfect patient experience. Lean is deployed not simply for quality improvement, but rather as an overall management strategy, coupled with an evolving institutional culture and focused invested leadership.

Elements on VMPS

VMPS is based on the application of Lean tools as part of a comprehensive management system together with institutional culture change and leadership focused on implementing change.

Lean Toolkit

The Lean toolkit has been discussed extensively in the medical literature, but can be summarized as a focus on the identification and elimination of waste from healthcare delivery processes. Waste is defined as any product or activity that does not add value for the patient.[7,8] Processes are standardized, and variability is reduced through dedicated 'Kaizen' quality improvement activities and Plan-Do-Study-Act cycles. Lean tools supporting these efforts include Value Stream Maps, Andon indicators for process control, Kanban cards for inventory control, and Jidoka or human supervised automation.[9] These Lean tools and events can lead to significant improvements in processes throughout the healthcare enterprises.[10,11,12] However, the Lean toolkit alone is insufficient for transformational change leading to sustainable success in improving quality and lowering costs.

Management System

Success in improving quality in a healthcare organization requires the understanding that quality improvement should not exist as an isolated silo or add-on, but must be the foundation for all management activities, including day-to-day operations. By identifying VMPS as a management system early on, we took 'project based', 'opt-in/opt-out', off the table. All activities from supply chain to operative procedures to primary care visits are based on VMPS value streams, and changes are effected through

Lean process improvement workshops and activities. In effect, all management activities are focused on quality improvement; doing the work becomes inseparable from improving the work. This required development of an educational infrastructure to train provider and staff at all levels complemented by a quality improvement division of specialists with deep expertise and fulltime work focusing on improvement. It should be emphasized, however, that the quality improvement specialists do not work in isolation but rather in collaboration with operational leaders who have also been through VMPS training.

As an example, to enable important early fluid resuscitation in patients with sepsis, we held a VMPS 2-day improvement event physically on an intermediate care unit, with front-line nurses, physicians and quality improvement specialist together contributing to immediate changes. By the conclusion of the event, the changes had become part of the day-to-day operations, with the improvement team now being the management team using the Lean toolkit for implementation. In this way, having VMPS as a management system provides the continuity to help address the challenge of sustaining improvements. Not every improvement proceeds from a formal workshop. Fundamental to VMPS is empowerment of and respect for the frontline workers, who are uniquely positioned to inspect for quality and contribute improvement ideas. Leaders are expected to convene daily team huddles on the work floor allowing for constructive bidirectional feedback. Further, all employees undergo basic Lean training, starting on the first day of work. It is not unusual to overhear conversations between staff, such as two transporters in the elevator talking about mistake-proofing their work.

Institutional Culture

Institutional culture is critically important[13] and probably the most elusive aspect of VMPS. Foundational to institutional culture is the shared vision that value to the patient is the focus of all activities. This does not mean simply that care is respectful and responsive to individuals, but rather, that all measures of quality (including efficiency, effectiveness, equity, safety, timeliness and outcomes) (3) are viewed from the perspective of the patient. In reality, most healthcare delivery is built around the needs of the doctors, nurses and managers, rather than around the needs of the patients. The simplest example of this is patient waiting rooms. Worldwide, we spend hundreds of millions of dollars building waiting rooms, so that patients can hurry up, be on time and wait for us in what are, in essence, large holding tanks. This extreme waste from the Lean perspective is the antithesis of efficient and timely care from the patient's perspective and representative of the scale of transformation required to truly become 'patient driven' in healthcare. Through VMPS, we have achieved incremental and breakthrough tangible gains in redesigning care around our patients, including opening a clinic with no waiting rooms, and reconstructing our care delivery for conditions like low back pain, headache and breast concerns around same day access and patient needs. Celebrating these patient-focused gains within the organization reinforces the VMPS institutional culture.

Physician culture at VM also had to adapt to the VMPS. Traditional models of healthcare delivery that feature physician hierarchies separate from that of nurses, support efficient patient-focused care. Customary physician expectations of autonomy, protection and entitlement can conflict with care quality, safety and patient-centeredness. To address physician culture, we engaged in a year process led by front-line physicians to formulate a new physician compact, a reciprocal agreement between providers and the organization.[14] Provider's responsibilities include implementing evidence-based practice, respecting all team members, and willingly embracing innovation and organizational change. Organizational responsibilities include providing tools and information necessary to improve practice, respecting all team members, and willingly embracing innovation and organizational change. Organizational responsibilities include providing tools and information necessary to improve practice, supporting career development and professional satisfaction, and being transparent about organizational priorities and business decisions. The compact defines the relationship between organizations and physicians and is incorporated into provider orientation, performance management and annual review.

Cultural change is not rapid, and requires constant commitment from leadership. Not everyone at VM was initially accepting of VMPS, and evolution in the institutional culture required time. There was resistance, particularly early on, to change in general, and to the concept of using a manufacturing approach in healthcare, as 'patients are not cars.' Acceptance increased gradually, prompted by trips to Japan and other industry visits for many leaders and by gradually increasing visibility of VMPS success. A small number of providers left as a consequence of VMPS, but at the same time, others came to VM specifically because of the institutional focus on quality and safety.

Leadership for Implementation

Leadership is required for a quality healthcare system. At its core, quality improvement is about change, and the large-scale and transformational changes required in healthcare can only be achieved with active, unwavering leadership. At Virginia Mason, the entire executive team, including the board of directions is required to undergo deep training in VMPS and to participate in training trips to Japan for in-depth study of Toyota and other Lean companies. All leaders undergo formal training in VMPS, and are expected to use the tools to lead events and to support teams, through daily management. This ensures consistency in leadership throughout the institution that is not dependent on any one individual.

VMPS also requires leaders to move from the 'hero mentality' of problem solvers of being coaches who build learning teams that use VMPS for long-term improvement. This implies a change from the usual physician or administrative leadership model with its silos and advocacy for one's own chain of control to transparency and system-thinking. At Virginia Mason, we developed a uniform 'standard work for leaders,' a series of tools and processes designed to improve communication between leaders and staff (daily huddles and leadership rounds), to increase the visibility of the daily work and goals (production boards and visual controls), to enable early identification of problems in daily work (dashboards and root cause analysis), and to improve accountability of leaders and staff (leadership checklists and Genba observations). All leaders learn standard work for leaders as part of their VMPS training, and the uniform application of these tools promotes transparency and accountability. As a consequence, teams learn to identify and solve problems on their own, and leader become managers of the system rather than problem solvers. The visibility of leaders deploying VMPS also contributes to the institutional culture.

Our journey was not without challenges. Early on, we focused too much on the Lean toolkit, and teams equated success with use of the tools alone. This misinterpretation led to overzealous regimentation by a few managers. We also overestimated the scale of change from a quality improvement event, expecting instant transformation rather than iterative improvement. Finally, we underestimated the challenges in leading people through change. Simply developing solutions in Lean quality improvement events did not equate with long-term improvements. Instead, to implement and sustain improvements, we rely on the key strategies discussed above through the institution (Table 1).

Conclusion

In the first decade the Lean journey at Virginia Mason we have succeeded in improving quality and lowering costs.[15] Even more importantly, however, we have demonstrated that Lean principles can be a structure for the transformational change needed in healthcare. Why then does Lean not work for everyone? Because simple changes from the use of the Lean toolkit in isolated quality improvement silos are not enough. Instead, transformation requires using Lean as part of a comprehensive management system in concert with institutional culture change and new leadership approaches to all aspects of healthcare delivery.

Table 1: Key strategies for Virginia Mason Production System (VMPS)

Key Strategies	Descriptions
Unrelenting focus on the patient	All activities are evaluated by whether or not they add value from the patient's perspective; a unifying shared vision
Uniform improvement method	A common language and approach used by all, for us, Lean
A strategic plan that serves as the organization's compass	A strategic plan is highly visible, presented at the start of all improvement and management meetings, with the relevance of that meeting to the strategic plan defined
Integration of daily management and quality improvement	The same teams and the same tools for daily management and quality improvement; in effect, all management is quality improvement, which is critical to sustaining gains
Leadership present on the shop floor, understanding and supporting teams	Leaders can best know what is going on in the organization, and can best coach and support teams when physically present where the work is occurring
Daily leader routines that are transparent and predictable	Leading by example requires standard work by leaders, and transparency promotes bidirectional accountability for managers and staff
Respect for people	All staff are empowered to contribute to improvement and all are valued for their contribution to the institution
Physician, leadership, and board compacts	Reciprocal agreements between the institution and physicians, leaders, and board members defining the responsibilities and expectations for all parties
A visual environment so one easily sees operational conditions	Work is made open and visible so that any problems become apparent and can be addressed in real time; production dashboards are publicly displayed
Long-term thinking	Constancy of purpose among leadership, ensuring continuity independent of specific individuals
Alignment	Alignment from the board of directors through frontline staff: all must understand the unwavering commitment to the patient focus and the VPMS method

[End reproduced article]

Why Lean Imperatives Fail

The article suggests that Lean transformation may fail if:

1. Lean is not part of a comprehensive management system;
2. Lean is not being utilized for institutional culture change;
3. new leadership approaches are not integrated into the Lean transformation process.

Table 2 contains failure modes related to Lean transformation imperatives in three areas: leadership, institutional culture change, and management systems, based on the article above (*Why Lean Doesn't Work for Everyone*).

Table 2: Failure Modes of Lean Imperatives

Leadership	
No Primary Focus	Leadership lacks a primary focus, which confuses decision-making, priorities, and problem-solving with multiple "best decisions" in any given scenario.
Not Linked to Strategy	If Lean isn't actively linked to strategy and not used to achieve strategy, Lean may fail.
Armchair Management	This implies that leaders get information and make decisions from behind a desk without going to see what is happening in the "real world."
Unpredictable or Missing Routines	Without routines, a Plan-Do-Check-Act (PDCA) mindset is not built into the fabric of the organization and Lean will fail.
Short-term Thinking Not Linked to Long-term Thinking	When short-term thinking is not linked to long-term thinking, actions for short-term wins can easily derail long-term wins.
Management System	
Multiple Improvement Languages	Multiple improvement languages lead to confusion and ultimately a lack of a single unified approach.
Misalignment	If the organization is not aligned to strategic objectives, operational priorities, top problems, etc., it will lead to confusion and mixed priorities throughout the organization.
Separating Daily Management and Improvement	Separating improvement from daily operations creates a "time to improve" and a "time to work."

Culture	
Lack of Respect	A culture that lacks respect or has an overwhelming neglect of mutual trust and respect will cause transformation to fail.
Politics	One or two members of a group with significant clout—e.g., a physician, board member, or senior leader—can easily derail a transformation for personal reasons.
Hidden Problems	Without visualization, problems become hidden and eat away at both culture and operations, causing Lean transformation to fail.

Leadership Style Challenges

A high-level leader from Toyota once said, "everything flows through TPS." This means, in part, that if Lean isn't actively used to achieve the company's strategy, Lean may fail or not achieve its fullest potential. Eventually, all leadership and management decisions must flow through the TPS-like system that the organization is architecting. Thus, the system becomes the framework for the style of leadership and management.

Not transforming leadership styles may perpetuate armchair management, meaning that leaders get information and make decisions from a desk and armchair without going to see the work being done. If leaders simply look at data on paper or act on information given to them in the office without routinely watching what people do, Lean may fail.

Without predictable and consistent routines, mid-level leaders and frontline workers may get mixed signals about what's important and the current priorities. If following a new policy is critical to achieving the strategy but there is no leader routine for checking and coaching to that standard, leaders may inadvertently communicate that the standard isn't important.

When leading, having multiple focus points with no primary focus point confuses decision-making, priorities, and problem-solving. Without clearly establishing who or what is the point of focus—e.g., the patient, the resident, the customer, the physician, or the owner—there are multiple "best decisions" in any given scenario.

Problems must be visible and clear, so they can be improved during operations and actions can be taken quickly. Predictable leadership routines linked with visual processes help improvement happen frequently as a part of operations as opposed to occurring at a separate time. When problems are hidden, not visualized, and not out in the open, they may never appear to leaders as problems, and thus may never be fixed. The people dealing with the problems, though, know they exist, and they eat away at culture and operational effectiveness, causing Lean transformation to fail. There must be a culture of transparency that ensures that problems are easily recognized and linked with leadership routines.

Management System Challenges

With every improvement methodology come a language and tool set. It is extremely difficult to find an organization or industry without an improvement methodology or improvement language. Rather than introducing a new language, practitioners should build upon existing knowledge within the industry and organization so that a Lean-like language can be integrated. Multiple improvement languages will lead to unnecessary internal competition and a lack of a single unified approach.

Language must not only be consistent but so too must be the strategic objectives, operational priorities, top problems, and initiatives within the organization. Misalignment will lead to confusion and mixed priorities. When senior leaders each go in different directions, it casts doubt throughout the organization about the true priorities.

Separating improvement and daily operations is another cause of confusion and Lean failure. Detaching improvement from daily operations creates a separate "time to improve" and "time to work." This perpetuates the firefighting mindset and separates root cause problem-solving from permanently fixing daily operational problems. In addition, week-long *kaizen* events without daily improvement integration create an atmosphere further separating improvement work from actual work.

Cultural Challenges

Every organization has politics and groups with more clout than others (e.g., boards, senior leaders, physician groups). Not having appropriate checks and agreements in place on how to handle certain behaviors, problems, and transformation techniques can easily lead to a lack of mutual trust and respect, undermining Lean transformation. One or two members of a group with significant clout (individual physicians, board members, or senior leaders) can easily take a transformation off track for personal and biased reasons.

A culture that lacks respect or has an overwhelming neglect of mutual trust and respect may cause transformation to fail. Many of the previous examples, including armchair management, politics, and short-term thinking, may violate mutual trust and respect. Having problems depicted visually and treated as opportunities for improvement, with predictable routines, from leaders who want to help solve problems, helps create a culture of mutual trust and respect.

Grasping the Business Case: Where to Start

As the authors discuss, beyond events and tools, Lean is about *organizational transformation*: a shift in culture, leadership, and management systems. Lean is not just improving processes and solving operational problems. Similarly, the former President of the Toyota Supplier Support Center Hajime Ohba said that many companies need a complete overhaul of management systems and culture to be successful, and process improvement alone is not enough. Despite this, many organizations choose only events and process improvements.[16]

Recognizing up front that Lean is not just a process improvement methodology is essential. Culturally, there are clashes between Lean-style traditional management systems and culture. As Emiliani discusses in the Foreword to this book, leaders must grasp early on that many Lean tools and concepts clash with most Western management systems and business cultures, so underlying norms can be challenged. Pushing complex concepts (i.e., TPS) through channels in the middle of an organization that is dominated by vastly different cultural paradigms, management systems, cultures, and principles than that of a Lean organization will result in minimal benefit and potentially failure.[17] The following excerpt[18] clearly demonstrates the importance of grasping the culture before starting Lean transformation:

> Lean implementation and sustainability is a key success factor for firms, as demonstrated by the TPS in particular[19,20,21,22,23]; however, societal culture can block improvement. Some companies failed to sustain lean implementations when they introduced these organizational concepts in the same way that they might introduce a new machine.[24,25] Without understanding the societal culture of the firm or the subsidiary where the implementation is introduced, sustaining the lean effort will fail.[26,27]
>
> For example, if organizations analyze and diagnose their current organizational and societal culture profiles before starting lean implementation, lean practitioners can determine where the basic cultural transformation should be focused. In other words, cultural transformation should be based on the outcomes of this diagnostic process. Also, if organizations learn the details of the required organizational and societal cultural changes for success, they will be more likely to improve their cultural profile based on those requirements and achieve high performance in lean practices. If the lean journey is constructed using a well-designed cultural transformation based on the diagnostic process, the probability of failure will be much lower.

Conclusion

Leaders may choose Lean to solve a specific problem, improve processes, or transform an organization. As the authors discuss, Lean doesn't work for everyone because simple Lean-like changes are not enough. Instead, "transformation requires using Lean as part of a comprehensive management system in concert with institutional culture change and new leadership approaches" to all aspects of the business.[28]

Prior to starting a Lean transformation, leaders should focus on diagnosing the current and desired organizational cultures and design the transformation based on this diagnostic process.

Table 3: Things to Consider When Choosing Lean Transformation[29]

Don't Choose Lean . . .	Do Choose Lean . . .
Only to improve processes and/or engage employees.	To improve processes and engage employees to transform your institutional culture, management systems, and leadership styles.
To position your organization only win an award.	To position your organization for long-term success.
Because you're in crisis mode and you waited too long to change.	Because you're choosing Lean at the right time to maintain current success and build more successes for the future.
To make fast, short-term, revolutionary changes to your business.	To incrementally transform based on urgency and skill for the long term.

CHAPTER 2

Starting Lean

Once an organization chooses to begin Lean with the imperatives of culture, leadership, and management systems, and it has diagnosed the current culture, it must then choose *how* and *where* it will begin.

The realm of transformation includes both revolutionary and incremental efforts. Revolutionary transformation happens much faster but takes more energy, time, money, and other resources. Incremental transformation takes longer but costs less and is more manageable for most organizations. For most organizations, Lean transformation via incremental organizational change will prove both more feasible and sustainable.[30]

Many Lean transformations have been initiated using four steps:

1. Identify a problematic process.
2. Map the current and future states.
3. Implement improvements.
4. Repeat.

This chapter gives detailed insight into how these four steps originated and the failure modes associated with them. Organizations have different starting points for Lean that are influenced by professional networks, forced changes by Toyota, and other successful organizations. Starting points are categorized into three mechanisms for institutional change:[31, 32]

- **Modeling:** This occurs when organizations like those in Toyota's network had a problem, searched for a solution, and utilized a TPS tool to solve it.

- **Professionalization:** This includes formal education, professional networks, and institutes that rapidly diffuse change models, creating groups with similar attributes and knowledge.

- **Forced Change:** This change occurs when an organization exerts pressure on other dependent organizations (like Toyota's suppliers) to enact change.

Modeling Challenges

Diffusion happens more quickly within Toyota's formal network than other formal networks because Toyota motivated network members to participate by heavily subsidizing it, creating conditions of participation, and maximizing knowledge transfer with defined processes.[33,34] In both the United States and Japan, Toyota used the innovations of supplier associations, consultants, and core group learning teams.

In Georgetown, KY, Toyota established a supplier association—the Bluegrass Automotive Manufacturers Association (BAMA)—to facilitate knowledge transfer from Toyota to its suppliers. Toyota then established the Toyota Supplier Support Center *(TSSC)* and sent well-trained consultants free of charge to suppliers to help solve problems. Eventually, Toyota created and maintained subnetworks to better learn by (for example) touring plants and having face-to-face contact *to* share knowledge.

Although TPS diffused knowledge to supplier organizations via the knowledge sharing network, it created a set of challenges to fully grasp and adapt TPS that still exists today, including ones related to the dilution and misunderstanding of Lean principles.[35]

Explicit knowledge sharing can happen quickly and may be easy to replicate.[36] With knowledge sharing networks and single elements of TPS, knowledge and Lean tools can spread very rapidly without an entire system. This allows a company to pick any element of a Lean system and attempt to implement it to solve a problem. Though cherry-picking Lean tools may solve a specific problem from time to time, eventually this approach will lead to a disjointed system of Lean tools at best and failure at worst.

Tacit knowledge sharing doesn't happen as quickly as explicit, but it has its own set of challenges. Some sharing of tacit knowledge may appear as cherry-picking because of its ease. Though cherry-picking tools may occasionally work in a silo, each element of a Lean system is linked to other elements. Without properly linking tools into a systematic approach, transformation may fail.

As an example of failed knowledge sharing, the General Motors plant in Lordstown, Ohio received a $1 billion investment in 1995 for a new facility where systems and processes didn't mesh as planned.[37] Essentially, GM used Lean elements, *andon* in particular, as a major component of the facility, attempting to increase productivity by 30%. Even with nearly a million hours of worker training, the visual signboards and processes of stopping the line wreaked havoc around the plant, severely hurting output. Eventually the andon system was removed.[38]

Professionalization Challenges

Since the term Lean was coined in 1988, the concept has been a part of professional networks, leading to both the diffusion and dilution of TPS. James Womack, founder of the Lean Enterprise Institute, suggests that starting transformation requires picking a value-creation process (i.e., a value stream), creating an A3 (a one-page summary of the project), running experiments, reflecting, and sharing with the rest of the organization.[39] This recommendation mirrors the outline in *Lean Thinking*, a follow up to *The Machine that Changed the World* on how to start Lean. In the book, Womack and Jones outline the phases, specific steps, and timeframe for the Lean journey. They state that within the first six months (i.e., getting started) the company should:[40]

1. find a change agent;

2. gain Lean knowledge;

3. find a lever (a crisis or problem);

4. map value streams;

5. begin kaikaku (radical/revolutionary change);

6. expand the scope of the change.

In 2013, years after the book was published, Womack noted the top misconceptions of the Lean movement, from his perspective, that may lead to Lean transformation failure.[41] The misconceptions are: Lean is about cost cutting; Lean is about factories; Lean happens within the walls of the company; and Lean is a process improvement methodology. Does the prescription for approaching the first six months in Lean actually give the false impression that Lean is solely a process improvement methodology?

ThedaCare, for example, established its primary mode of Lean as kaizen or rapid improvement events after visiting Ariens.[42] Ariens marked its first kaizen event in late 2000, and had over 150 kaizen events within three years. ThedaCare, taking the same pathway, realized years later that it was asking everyone else to change but not changing its own leadership styles and management systems. Of course, any Lean transformation takes a long time, but it took over a decade for ThedaCare to realize the importance of leadership and management systems after imitating an event-based pathway to transformation.[43]

Kaizen events are complex tools in the Lean tool box that must be introduced at an appropriate time, when the organization is ready. Most organizations, like the GM Lordstown plant, attempt to utilize complex tools like kaizen events and andon too early, before the culture, management systems, and leadership styles are in place to both support and sustain them.

The last misconception that Womack discusses is that Lean is used by frontline workers to improve process and isn't used by management to actually change the enterprise. One of the factors that may have led to the misconception of Lean being a process improvement methodology and focused on finance is the recommendation from Lean gurus to essentially start by mapping and improving processes, which in many cases has been the primary mode of Lean transformation (or lack thereof). Coincidently, the proposed approach is nearly identical to that used by the Toyota Supplier Center.

Forced Change Challenges

In 1992, Toyota founded the Toyota Supplier Support Center (TSSC) to provide training in TPS to its suppliers and those of other North American companies. The operation of TSSC was based on Toyota's internal Operations Management Consulting Division (OMCD) in Japan.[44] The purpose of the OMCD was to give Toyota's employees the opportunity to solve complex problems through teaching, training, and coaching, by leading improvement activities in this fashion (note the similarities between the TSSC approach and the "Getting Started" approach outlined in *Lean Thinking*):[45]

1. Establish the topic, theme, or general subject matter for improvement.
2. Implement kaizen improvement activities.
3. Repeat implementation using trial and error until the targeted operational and business results are achieved.
4. Present a summary of results.
5. Conduct a final evaluation of comments by Toyota's OMCD department.[46]

One of the first general managers of TSSC, Hajime Ohba, recognized the discrepancy between traditional North American organizations and Toyota: "It takes a very long time and tremendous commitment to implement the Toyota Production System. In many cases, it takes a total cultural and organizational change. Many U.S. firms have management systems that contradict where you need to go."[47]

Challenges to the Toyota Supplier Approach

Toyota, via its supplier support center, does not focus on changing management systems, institutional culture, or leadership styles at supplier organizations—it takes a non-interventional approach.[48] Despite this, many organizations over the last several decades have used the Toyota supplier and TSSC approaches in attempting to become Lean.

Although Toyota wants positive supplier relationships, the focus is on *interfacing* with suppliers, not *intervening*. Toyota does not force its managerial values onto suppliers and its approaches are not transformational.

Transactional requirements that Toyota places on its suppliers are primarily technical and include: [49]

- Focus on improving specific processes
- Tracking the number of kaizen events
- Tracking and monitoring downtime with a standard approach to recovery plans
- Reviewing quality problems daily
- A comprehensive approval process for major kaizen
- Positive supplier development relationships
- Cost-reduction activities

Toyota does not require its suppliers to have:[50]

- A focus on complete systems
- Total preventative maintenance
- *Gemba* walks and shop floor management activities
- Tracking of the organization's overall goals and metrics
- Approval for minor kaizen
- A focus on human aspects and the soft side of TPS
- Toyota's managerial values
- Employee relations

The diffusion and professionalization of Lean has largely been influenced by The Toyota Supplier Support Center within Toyota's network. Replicating this largely transactional approach over a transformation approach leads to a number of different barriers to Lean transformation.

Toyota emphasizes improving specific processes that directly impact Toyota's supply chain using kaizen events. Because it's the first method of improvement Toyota used on many suppliers, many believe that it is the best way to start any transformation, whether linked to Toyota's supply chain or not. The kaizen event, though, is a complex tool that must link to other tools within TPS. Starting with kaizen events may have been appropriate for Toyota's suppliers, but it is generally not the best approach for an organization undergoing a transformation.

Additionally, Toyota tracks the number of kaizen events for suppliers, both major and minor kaizen, to control and monitor the improvements and the impact on quality. Many organizations adapting TPS choose to monitor the number of kaizen events as a means of measuring the success of "becoming lean." The number of kaizens, however, is not an indication of how well the organization is achieving its strategy and results and should not be a number to measure the success of transformation. Tracking it, in many cases, only perpetuates the misconception that running kaizen events is the primary mode of Lean transformation, which it is not.

Regarding kaizen with Toyota's suppliers, there is a comprehensive approval process for major kaizen and little to no approval process for minor kaizen. Some organizations misunderstand kaizen, believing that there is no sophisticated approval process. This has led leaders to believe that TPS is primarily a grassroots, frontline engagement technique that leadership must support but does not necessarily lead. This, of course, will lead to Lean failure.

Toyota focuses on the technical aspects of TPS, over its human aspects and soft side, with its suppliers. In general, the Lean community was initially misled toward the technical elements of TPS over human elements.[51] Tools such as *kanban*, andon, 5S, value stream mapping, TQM, and others were the initial focus of the Lean movement and lack a focus on people.

Similarly, when interfacing with its suppliers, Toyota focuses on cost reduction activities and not necessarily people development within suppliers. For example, Toyota does not require employee suggestion systems and does not require means of stabilizing employee relations at suppliers. This may have influenced the emphasis within the Lean community on cost reduction activities over people development activities at the beginning of the Lean movement, which was well acknowledged by academics decades later.

The lack of emphasis on people development includes a non-interventional approach to leadership styles at Toyota's suppliers. Toyota requires its suppliers to review quality problems daily but does not require gemba walks and shop floor management activities. This ensures that quality problems impacting Toyota are resolved quickly but does not specify *how* problems are resolved. Therefore, if the organization has a command and control style of leadership, that style can continue as long as quality problems are addressed.

All in all, the interactions between Toyota and its suppliers serve the transactional purpose of changing specific outcomes of suppliers that directly impact Toyota. The non-interventional, non-transformational approaches initially used by TSSC served Toyota well, but these approaches are not best suited for transformation. To an extent, professionalization of Lean has resulted in a homogeneous Lean community with legitimation by both university specialists and growth of professional networks where the Lean knowledge has diffused quickly, which has led to the dilution of TPS.[52]

Using Lean to solve specific problems or improve processes isn't wrong, but if the purpose is transformation, using Lean as a process improvement methodology or cherry-picking elements is not *transformational*. Generally, mapping a process and improving that process are also not transformational in the sense of culture, management systems, and leadership. Additionally, many experienced individuals may promise to change culture, leadership, and management systems, but execute based on the TSSC approach or the approach outlined in *Lean Thinking* due to professionalization and misunderstanding of long-term organizational transformation.

Getting Started

Start with leadership, because the senior team's culture is typically the most dominant within the organization, essentially defining the corporate culture. Changing a nondominant culture without changing leadership's culture may be a fruitless effort.[53]

Establishing a frontline pilot area to transform alongside leadership begins to link frontline processes and team members to the strategy of the organization. If done properly, this approach simultaneously begins to create a counterculture (a subculture different than the dominant culture of the organization) of mutual trust and respect that eventually infiltrates the entire organization. The pilot, then, becomes a place to see the new culture and to demonstrate to the rest of the organization what the future holds. Rather than focusing on improving an organizational process, focus on creating the new management system, leadership styles, and culture within a pilot hall or business unit of the organization. Then leaders can learn from and spread the system, which, as discussed in the next chapter, has a different set of barriers.[54]

Conclusion

Lean has been largely influenced by academics writing about mature Lean organizations and practitioners heavily influenced by TSSC-like approaches to solving problems and improving processes. Selecting a starting point can be difficult, so understanding the history behind different approaches may help an organization choose.

Toyota requires non-interventional concepts for its suppliers, meaning the TSSC approach to Lean is most likely not the best approach to incremental organizational transformation. Similarly, the starting point recommended by Womack and Jones may also not be the best approach due to inserting complex concepts into an organization without the culture, management systems, and leadership styles in place to support the process changes. Organizations can avoid a false start by starting with the leadership and a frontline pilot area.

Table 4: Things to Consider When Starting Lean Transformation

Don't Start Lean by . . .	Do Start Lean by . . .
Imitating or copying tools from other organization.	Learning how other organizations struggled and planning to avoid pitfalls.
Simply running kaizen events, getting results, and repeating.	Having a multi-year adapted plan for transformation.
Choosing a consultant or internal coach based on promised results.	Evaluating the pathway from consultants and coaches.
Focusing on one process that spans the entire organization to improve.	Focusing on a small subset of the organization, a pilot hall, to see the system working.

CHAPTER 3

Learning from the Pilot Area

If the transformation journey leads to initial success in the pilot area, the learnings must be spread throughout the organization, which has its own set of barriers. For this chapter, I chose two discussions. The first focuses on understanding the diffusion of Lean within the healthcare sector from the standpoint of physicians who may have benefited from being exposed to a successful TPS-like pilot. The second article and discussion are from a well-known pilot area, New United Motor Manufacturing Incorporated (NUMMI), discussing the barriers to knowledge transfer.

Challenges Transitioning to Healthcare

In 2016, leaders of the Lean community criticized two physicians (and best-selling authors) who were very critical of Lean, instead of learning from and conducting a root cause analysis on these physicians' valid (yet sometimes misguided) arguments.[55,56]

In the New England Journal of Medicine (NEJM), physicians Pamela Hartzband and Jerome Groopman published *Medical Taylorism*, a title that refers to Frederick Taylor who is known as the father of scientific management and one of the first efficiency experts in manufacturing. The authors pointed out many positives brought on by TPS in healthcare, including:

- Standardized protocols reducing hospital-acquired infections
- Timely care for stroke patients
- Timely care for myocardial infarction patients

However, the primary argument of the article is that Taylorism and TPS cannot be applied to "many vital aspects of medicine," the authors saying that:

"The aim of finding the one best way cannot be generalized to all of medicine, least of all, to many key cognitive tasks. Good thinking takes time, and the time pressure of Taylorism creates a fertile field for cognitive errors that can result in medical mistakes." (p. 107)

The points they outline against Lean, TPS, and Taylorism include the following:

- Patients following standardized processes like those deployed in automobile manufacturing
- Electronic health records promoting the "one best way" to encounters
- Patients given checklists in an effort to streamline the process (which is not patient-centric)
- Managers use stopwatches in emergency departments and clinics to measure the duration of patient visits
- Rushed and at times unnecessary protocols ignore patients' preferences
- New medical students are inappropriately conditioned that there is "one best way" to diagnose and treat

The authors close with the argument that:

"Good medical care takes time, and there is no one best way to treat many disorders. When it comes to medicine, Taylor was wrong: 'man' must be first, not the system." (p. 108).

From the last chapter, we learned that many Lean transformations have been initiated using four steps:

1. Identify a problematic process.
2. Map the current and future states.
3. Implement improvements.
4. Repeat.

The fruits of those process improvements have yielded many positives despite a lack of full integration into the existing culture of both the industry and the organization, many of which can be read about in any Lean book. However, some negative unintended consequences, including the arguments outlined in *Medical Taylorism*,[57] accompany those fruits.

As discussed in the last chapter, Lean practitioners and leaders of organizations are misguided into jumping into process improvement first, which is the approach advocated by Womack and Jones in *Lean Thinking* and was the primary method used by TSSC for Toyota's suppliers. Using stopwatches, creating inappropriate checklists, and rushing physicians are most definitely byproducts, even if unintended, of Lean as a process improvement methodology.

Below is a summary of the problem and a very basic root cause analysis:

Problem: Authors argue against Lean, TPS, and Taylorism.

Why? Partially due to streamlining physician-patient interactions leading to errors.

Why? Streamlining processes in many cases is a directive from leadership and/or Lean practitioners.

Why? The current standard from Lean community leaders is to start with process improvement for a Lean transformation.

The next argument from the authors is discussed in the closing: "man" must be first and not the system. This may again be misguided, but may be valid, and should be analyzed. Virtually all the adaptations of TPS in healthcare that I have read, visited, or even coached have been based on a patient-centric model that puts the patient first. I believe an argument by the authors is that a Lean system should put the physician first, so the physician can put the patient first ("man" first). That is, ensuring that the physician has all the information quickly to discuss options and understand what's really happening with the patient. Putting the physician in the driver's seat of a patient-first model may reduce errors that can be caused or accelerated by streamlining processes.

In a separate article, the same physicians/authors discuss the "3A errors": anchoring, availability, and attribution.[58] Anchoring is when the physician or problem-solver fixates on a particular bit of information and continues to think linearly down that one path of investigation, missing other key pieces of information. Availability is when the physician or problem-solver jumps to what seem to be similar cases and draws conclusions about a new case based on those similar cases too quickly. Attribution is when the physician or problem-solver focuses on the characteristics of the person or stereotypes such as "suffering from old age," when that is actually not the case for the individuals' ailments. All of these errors may increase speed but are ultimately still errors.

Clearly, the authors' opinion is that over-streamlining processes and overemphasizing the "one best way" approach only exacerbates the 3A errors when it comes to appropriately diagnosing patients. Transporting TPS from automobile manufacturing to healthcare has proven a challenge, as demonstrated by the case studies in this book. TPS is not transportable and must be adapted to not only the organization but the industry. Transporting TPS from one automobile manufacturer to another, even under the best of circumstances, has proven to be equally difficult.

NUMMI: A Joint Pilot

The joint venture between Toyota and General Motors in Freemont, CA, known as the New United Motor Manufacturing, Inc. (NUMMI), was a tremendous learning opportunity for both GM and Toyota. Many organizations experience extreme difficulties in taking advantage of learning alliances, and GM was no different. Therefore, I chose an excerpt from *Learning through Alliances* to highlight the barriers GM experienced when learning from Toyota and transferring the knowledge from NUMMI to the rest of General Motors.

At NUMMI, the goals for General Motors were to learn the Toyota Production System first-hand while producing a small car to compete with the Japanese.[59] Specifically, General Motors also wanted its managers to see teamwork, elimination of waste, and high-quality production up close and in person, learning from Toyota.[60]

The main purposes for Toyota were both human and operational: rapid entry to the US market and learning how to work with an American workforce.[61] Within one year, the NUMMI plant went from a "bad" culture producing the worst quality within GM to a culture of mutual trust and respect producing the best quality in GM.[62]

At NUMMI, 2,500 workers assembled the Chevrolet Nova, Toyota Corolla, and GEO Prizm. General Motors was responsible for providing the facility and selling the cars, while Toyota was responsible for design, operations, and production management. Because Toyota managed NUMMI, it took full responsibility for mentoring the American workforce, with direction coming straight from the top of Toyota. GM, however, initially struggled with learning.

Learning Challenges at NUMMI

Barriers to transferring knowledge generally acquired via Toyota at NUMMI included those related to causal ambiguity, leadership commitment, the cost of learning, individual managers as the learning conduit, and "not invented here" syndrome.[63] These challenges, and a brief explanation of each, are shown in Table 5 and described in a later section.[64]

Table 5: Barriers to Transferring Knowledge from the Pilot to the Rest of the Organization

Barriers	**Meaning**
Causal ambiguity	Managers/leaders do not understand how organizational actions and outcomes relate.
Leadership commitment	Leaders should be catalysts and architects, with a focus on learning rather than ownership/structural issues.
Cost of learning	Intense deep learning versus merely exposing individuals to new knowledge.
Individual managers as the learning conduit	Managers are expected to transfer knowledge, but there's no organizational plan behind the transfer.
"Not invented here" syndrome	The misconception that ideas developed in other organizations aren't as good as the ones developed within the organization.

The following excerpt discusses the initial learning struggles at General Motors, as well as the steps GM took to overcome knowledge transfer barriers.

Article 2: "Learning Through Alliances: General Motors and NUMMI."

Andrew Inkpen

GM's Initial Struggles with Learning

GM's attempt to transfer knowledge in the mid-1980s was driven by the realization that NUMMI was outperforming comparable GM plants. However, the first few waves of advisors moved from NUMMI to GM were largely unsuccessful in their efforts to transfer knowledge. One problem was that managers assigned to NUMMI in the early years of the joint venture were given little preparation or training for their assignment. One manager sent to NUMMI in 1986 had one month to prepare and was told by his boss in Detroit to "learn as much as you can." When these managers' assignments were completed, normally after two years, they were expected to return to GM to share their experience. However, although the NUMMI advisors were learning as individuals, many became frustrated when they re-entered GM because they were unable to implement the ideas they had learned from NUMMI. This difficulty with implementation was driven by two factors. The first was significant resistance within GM and a lack of understanding as to how GM could benefit from lean manufacturing. Although some GM executives saw an opportunity to learn from Toyota, many senior managers were opposed and even resented the idea of collaborating with a Japanese company. These managers were essentially in denial, attributing the Japanese automakers success to unfair competition (low value of the yen, government support in Japan, and so on) rather than better management. Under these circumstances, which persisted until about 1992, system-wide learning was impossible.

The lack of understanding and appreciation for the value of NUMMI knowledge ties back to the discussion of causal ambiguity. Knowledge cannot be appropriately valued if it cannot be understood. Knowledge associated with the TPS was particularly difficult to understand because of its systemic and integrated nature, which leads to a second factor impacting the implementation of NUMMI ideas. Within GM there was a belief that the "secret" to the TPS was observable and transportable, i.e., "if we could just get the blueprints for stamping." However, the knowledge was not easily broken down into transportable pieces. The knowledge about the TPS and lean manufacturing was deeply embedded in the Toyota context and was tied into an integrated system.[65] As a manager said, "You cannot cherry pick elements of lean manufacturing; you must focus on the whole system. Once you learn how the system works you need a good understanding of the philosophy that underpins it." The initial learning challenges are summed up in the following statement from a GM manager:

> "We [managers in GM] started with denial that there was anything to learn. Then we said Toyota is different, so it won't work at GM. Eventually we realized there was something to learn. The leaders initially said: implement lean manufacturing, but they did not understand it... We went to Japan and saw *kanban* and *andon*, but people did not understand why they work. We did not understand that the TPS is an integrated approach and not just a random collection of ideas... We implemented parts of the system but did not understand that it was the system that made the difference. . . We did not understand that the culture and behavior had to change before the techniques would have an impact."

By the mid- to late-1980s pockets of support for using NUMMI as a learning vehicle were emerging within GM. However, the North American manufacturing organization was largely opposed to a joint venture with Toyota and was confident in its own abilities. Many advisors who were moved to such an environment found that they had limited influence on the beliefs and norms of the new GM unit to which they were assigned. Those that were able to make an impact had to persevere and accept that in the early days of learning from NUMMI, implementation of lean ideas would mean limited recognition and rewards.

There were other learning missteps. From 1990 to 1995 GM did extensive videotaping of NUMMI operations with the expectation that the videotapes could be used to illustrate the TPS. The problem was that the videotapes could only show how the TPS worked and not why, which meant only surface learning could happen. GM also tried to quickly implement some of the obvious TPS elements, such as *andon* systems. An *andon* refers to the warning lights on an assembly line that signal work center status. In the *andon* system the operator can signal the team leader when there is a problem. The worker pulls the cord once to sound an alarm to get the team leader's attention. If the cord is not pulled again within 60 seconds, the line will stop. For GM, the idea of allowing line workers to stop the line was revolutionary. In trying to implement *andon*, GM initially failed because they did not understand the non-visible processes that supported *andon*, such as standardized work, team member systems, and problem solving.[66] As one former plant manager said, "I was not successful in implementing *andon* because we did not really understand what it would take to make it work." Whereas GM interpreted the *andon* system as "when you pull the cord the line will stop," Toyota developed *andon* so the operator could get help when needed and to ensure the line kept moving at the optimal speed and to ensure that problems were solved when they occurred. Only rarely will the entire assembly line stop at Toyota, whereas GM initially saw *andon* as problematic because it could lead to line stoppages, which in the mass production mentality is the worst thing that can happen. Ironically, GM initially focused on TPS elements associated with visual control (such as *andon)* because the elements were visible and obvious to anyone seeing the TPS for the first time. However, the key lessons of the visual control elements were not visible and required deep understanding of the TPS.

A Learning System Emerges

In 1992, a pivotal event occurred. Jack Smith was appointed as CEO and played a key role in changing the leadership orientation towards NUMMI. Jack Smith headed the GM negotiating team when NUMMI was formed and understood that the joint venture created a major learning opportunity. Smith became the head of European operations in 1987, vice chairman for international operations in 1990, CEO of GM in 1992, and chairman in 1996. In Europe, Smith built a team of colleagues that recruited people who understood lean production, many of whom who had experience in NUMMI. With Jack Smith as CEO, learning from NUMMI became a priority for GM (although vestiges of the denial lingered on for years). The following describes the key mechanisms that supported learning and knowledge transfer.

The Technical Liaison Office

In 1985, GM created the NUMMI Technical Liaison Office (TLO) in Freemont. The TLO's task is to manage and document learning and disseminate knowledge from NUMMI to GM. From 1985 to 2003, the scope of the TLO expanded to incorporate a wide variety of training and knowledge transfer activities. More specifically, after 1992, significant changes were made in how the TLO supported learning. The TLO is staffed by a small number of full-time employees and, like NUMMI itself, has a group of 10-11 advisors on assignment from GM. These advisors have the same structured learning requirement as the advisors in NUMMI although TLO advisors spent more time on teaching activities than advisors assigned to the plant.

The TLO is involved in both knowledge transfer from NUMMI to GM and knowledge change within GM. The TLO coordinates the multi-year advisor pro- grams and other shorter visits, including the following:

- Study teams focused on learning about a specific task (such as how to build doors), the TLO designs a learning experience of 3 days to 2 weeks, and teams must establish an implementation team and follow-up;
- Short awareness visits and plant tours (1-2 days);
- Short-term assignments (2 weeks);
- Executive in residence (8 months), one executive at a time; and
- Topical workshops (3-5 days) on topics such as recognition and rewards, which may be broadcast to other GM sites.

The TLO supports the documentation of TPS knowledge, which makes the knowledge more easily teachable and transferable. The TLO also performs training designed to educate GM managers about the potential impact the TPS could have on GM manufacturing. Finally, in recent years the TLO has expanded its activity base to include a consulting business primarily focused on NUMMI and GM suppliers.

[End of excerpt from Inkpen, Andrew. *California Management Review* (47 no. 4) pp. 114-136, copyright © 2005 by SAGE Publications, Inc.]

Reproduced by Permission of SAGE Publications, Inc.

Overcoming Knowledge Transfer Challenges

Strong parallels exist between the NUMMI-GM diffusion of TPS within General Motors and other organizations' learning of Lean. For example, many academics and practitioners of Lean and operational excellence grasp the immense theoretical benefits of these practices within organizations and industries. However, these same individuals find it extremely difficult or even impossible to successfully implement the systematic ideas behind TPS/Lean, much like those from NUMMI did when returning to General Motors. Grasping the barriers that GM and other organizations have faced helps leaders design actions to overcome current and potential barriers. The barriers and potential actions to counter them are summarized in Table 6.[67]

Table 6: Knowledge Transfer Barriers and Countermeasures to Adapting TPS

Barriers	Actions and Countermeasures
Causal ambiguity	Grasp that TPS is not transportable. Enforce behaviors. Have a sensei.
Leadership commitment	Executive leaders must be architects of the system. Have a systematic plan. Promote leaders that embody the system.
Individual managers as the learning conduit	Create a learning system and office.

"Not invented here" syndrome	Integrate knowledge into existing practices. Establish a pilot.
The cost of learning	Leverage learning as early as possible. Actively and continually improve knowledge transfer.

Managers and leaders don't know what actions to imitate in order to replicate outcomes and results, which is called causal ambiguity.[68] TPS is very difficult to understand, given both the underlying culture of Toyota and the comprehensive and integrated systems that can't be seen and described easily, let alone replicated. Not understanding how outcomes and actions relate also causes Lean leaders to emphasize the wrong actions to try to transport TPS.

Leaders must grasp that TPS is not all observable and transportable, meaning that the organization can't simply "do Lean tools" in order to become a Lean organization. John Shook, author and former employee at NUMMI, states that changing behavior changes thinking, thereby changing values and attitudes and eventually culture. He compares this to the old model, which is changing thinking to change behavior.[69] Leaders must focus on changing and aligning behavior, which will result in changed thinking. Lean tools, then, become fruits of changed thinking. A true sensei will understand not only how TPS works within a mature organization but how to sequence the behaviors to reap the fruits of changed thinking.

Many leaders, when it comes to Lean, want to delegate to a set of experts instead of actually leading transformation. This not only leads to a lack of ownership by leadership, it leads to the Lean experts not properly linking the Lean system to the strategy. To overcome these barriers, leaders must take time up front to architect, learn, and own the systematic approach to transformation. Leaders must ensure that the Lean system aligns with the strategy of the organization and that all decisions flow through the system from both a strategic and operational standpoint.

Another problem with spreading Lean is individual managers as the learning conduit. This occurred with Toyota and General Motors when GM simply sent managers to NUMMI and said "learn as much as you can" with no systematic approach to knowledge capture, knowledge transfer, and relationship building. In many cases, managers are expected to transfer knowledge, but there's no organizational plan or support behind the transfer. The organization must not only help managers be successful, it must provide learning conduits—systems and processes—for further transformational learning.

Knowledge diffusion and transfer is not a single objective but rather an ongoing objective to be actively managed and improved. Creating a learning liaison office and learning processes can help facilitate learning in order to further spread Lean transformation. A learning office also helps alleviate "not invented here" syndrome, because best practices are actively shared. This syndrome is defined when something such as a product or system that was developed somewhere else is considered not as good as one that the company develops itself.[70]

In many cases, organizations are not willing to incur the seemingly large cost of a learning system compared to the lower cost of exposure and training. Inkpen demonstrates the difference between Toyota and General Motors at the time of NUMMI: Toyota sent engineers to NUMMI with no defined tasks or purposes, simply to learn and observe.[71] In contrast, GM had much more specific tasks assigned (e.g., videotape a process in order to replicate it) that actually led to less learning of the systematic approach behind TPS.

Many managers at NUMMI came back to GM and met resistance to implementing the new ideas in TPS. Successful knowledge transfer of TPS means both giving knowledge and actually changing the knowledge of the receiver. In other words, simply preaching TPS or implementing tools is not enough for learning to occur—knowledge needs to be diffused within an organization or most of its individuals for transformational learning to occur.

To overcome this barrier, an organization should leverage learning as early as possible, actively and continually improve knowledge transfer, and focus on people over databases. Though Inkpen specifically discusses the transfer of knowledge within an alliance, learning must occur within the organization as TPS begins to develop as a form of knowledge transfer.[72]

Rather than having concrete objectives for knowledge diffusion of

TPS tools, organizations should establish an ongoing knowledge sharing process. A process will promote learning and continuous improvement above one-time transfer of knowledge. General Motors, for example, created the Technical Liaison Office and an advisor system. It also used greenfield plants, such as the Opel division, to showcase Lean manufacturing. Before attempting to diffuse TPS throughout an organization, those charged with the task should identify how knowledge will be transferred on an ongoing basis rather than taking a one-time approach.

Additionally, General Motors promoted leaders from within NUMMI to higher-level positions within GM. Promoting the leaders who embody the system gives positive reinforcement to the organization about who gets promoted and why. Furthermore, eventually these leaders will infiltrate management to the point where the organizational culture will dramatically shift.

GM attempted to integrate TPS with existing elements within it and eventually called the system the *Global Manufacturing System (GMS)*. This was aimed at helping General Motors internalize and own a TPS-like system. Exposing all the problems of the organization without recognizing the current positives that align with TPS may cause leaders to shut down and resist any continual efforts to adapt TPS.

In many cases, GM waited too long to learn from NUMMI. GM's adaptation of TPS and learning from NUMMI could have been far greater had it happened much earlier. Regardless, understanding and grasping these lessons will help organizations learn from and develop approaches to adapting and diffusing TPS throughout their organizations and networks. Before starting or reinvigorating a plan for TPS integration, ensure that there is a learning system established from the onset to promote and leverage learning continuously and as early as possible.

Conclusion

As previously stated multiple times throughout this book, when adapting TPS, do not start as a process improvement methodology first. Lean leaders and healthcare leaders must focus on creating an interlinked system. If General Motors, under the full direction of Toyota, couldn't spread the learnings from NUMMI back into General Motors easily, do we really believe that healthcare organizations have successfully adapted TPS as a methodology for organizational transformation that can be replicated?

Establishing a transformational model within the organization is difficult, but, spreading those learnings via knowledge management processes and systems has its own set of barriers. As the extension of Lean transformation continues, the roll-out process has a different set of barriers that must be overcome in order for Lean transformation to prevail.

Table 7: Things to consider when spreading Lean

When Spreading Lean Don't. . .	When Spreading Lean Do. . .
Expect the entire organization or entire business unit to transform at once.	Select a pilot area to adapt the transformation plan.
Expect managers to learn Lean and adapt it themselves.	Have a learning and knowledge sharing process.
Expect that Lean transformation will be transportable from area to area within your business.	Promote leaders from the pilot area as a mechanism to spread transformation.
Have Lean experts architect the roll-out plan.	Have senior leadership under the guidance of Lean experts architect the roll-out plan.

CHAPTER 4

Extending Transformation

Once transformational imperatives, strategies, and requirements are established, and a model area with knowledge transfer systems and processes is in place, generally the next step in Lean transformation is spreading and extending it to the rest of the organization. This step in the Lean transformation process brings a different set of challenges that must be managed appropriately.

In this chapter, I selected an excerpt about one of the largest Lean healthcare experiments to date—in the Canadian province of Saskatchewan—and the reasons for its failure. At the end of the excerpt, the author provides a Strengths, Weaknesses, Opportunities, and Threats (SWOT) analysis on the roll-out of Lean in Saskatchewan, and I further dissect the causes of the failure.

I also chose to use an excerpt from *Rolling Out Lean Production Systems* to highlight success factors and challenges of rolling-out Lean that are applicable to any sector. Some challenges are actually counterintuitive to what many Lean practitioners may recommend. After the article, I provide more specific examples and explanations of these failure modes.

The Saskatchewan Lean Transformation

In 2011, the Saskatchewan Party government began what one expert called "the biggest experiment in health transformation in the world."[73] An experienced consulting group, John Black Associates, introduced Lean transformation with a four-year, $40-million contract.[74]

The first project was an exercise to cut $50 million from the first children's hospital in the province.[75] By the end of the contract, after just under four years, 440 Rapid Process Improvement Workshops (RPIWs),

20 waves of Lean Leader trainings, 22 Production Preparedness Process (3P) events, 13 kanban seminars, 4 5S (workplace organization) train-the-trainer sessions, and 42 reviews were completed.[76]

Though many successes using Lean have been documented in Saskatchewan, by November 2014, the political and media coverage became "increasingly hostile to Lean and John Black Associates."[77] The following article, *Rolling-out Lean in Saskatchewan Health Care System*, begins to explain the causes for this increased hostility.

Article 3: "Rolling-out Lean in the Saskatchewan Health Care System: Politics Derailing Policy"

Tom McIntosh

Factors that Influences the Roll-Out Decision

The planned roll-out of Saskatchewan's Lean initiatives to encompass the entirety of the system was clearly driven from within the Ministry of Health and, in particular, with the enthusiastic support of Dan Florizone, the Deputy Minister of Health from 2008 until 2013.[78] It was not about putting the issue onto the government's agenda, but rather taking the next step after applying Lean to the internal operations of the Ministry and the Regional Health Authorities (RHAs). The challenge in this part of the Lean implementation was that it would directly engage with a variety of new stakeholders, namely those who delivered care and their representatives.

Saskatchewan governments have historically had a generally positive relationship with the Saskatchewan Medical Association (SMA) and the Saskatchewan Registered Nurses Association (SRNA).[79] Likewise, the Saskatchewan Party government has had a generally positive relationship with the Saskatchewan Union of Nurses (SUN) which had experienced quite open conflict with the previous New Democratic Party government.

So, there is reason to believe that the government did not foresee a significant difference between implementing Lean in the "back office operations" of the health system and its full-scale introduction into the health system proper. Their internal belief seems to have been that what had been a success on the bureaucratic and administrative side would be equally successful on the care delivery side. And though they would later disavow Lean, SUN admits to being optimistic about its implementation in care settings at the outset.[80]

But with each of these factors there are warning flags that failed to be acknowledged. First, there is neither publicly available data that confirms the government's insistence that Lean's implementation has been a success nor any independent evaluation of cost-savings or efficiencies implemented. Second, the generally positive relationship between the government and the health professions always rested on the government's acknowledgement of and respect for the autonomy and authority of those professions within the system and, especially, at the point of care. Lean calls for a reorganization of the health care hierarchy and for an opening up of decision-making and thus, by its nature, raises at the very least the potential for conflict with professional autonomy.

What is not particularly clear is how Lean and patient-centeredness can be applied simultaneously in an environment with multiple centers of power and decision-making authority. That is, Lean applied to manufacturing involves delegating (but not devolving) authority down the hierarchy to encourage innovation to flow upward. But health care in Canada lacks the hierarchical structures of a factory. The Ministry of Health holds certain authority (and the purse strings) but the professions, especially medicine and nursing, maintain professional and regulatory autonomy that predate Lean and which historically governments have not impinged on lightly. To the extent these professions saw their autonomy threatened, they were prepared to push back against the government's plans.

How the Implementation Failed (or was Stalled)

The roll out of Lean to more and more of the health care system began to raise issues about how committed these key professions were to changes that might be seen to compromise their autonomy in the decisions around the delivery of care. In a posting on the

SUN website the union president explained their disenchantment:

> Now that Lean is being put into practice we are seeing the primary focus is on creating efficiencies, waste reduction and budgetary savings only, it fails to take into account patient acuity and complexity and is unfortunately proving to have little impact on direct care at the bedside and patient outcomes. ...The fact is we are finding that Lean does not fit with the registered nursing process, safe nursing practice, registered nurse decision-making or the formulation of nursing diagnoses. Lean is viewing important knowledge-based aspects of registered nursing, such as consultations, as wasted time. The linear, production-line approach to creating efficiencies does not take into account the flexibility needed to deal with increasing and evolving complexities and acuities of patients we are seeing today.[81]

As Poksinska (2010) has noted, Lean implementation in health care can (or can be seen to) compromise professional autonomy and therefore meet strong resistance from health professionals.[82] Unlike its application to the back-office operations of the health authorities, Lean's implementation at the point of care depends on the consent and participation of a variety of stakeholders whose authority within the health system is independent of the Ministry itself. To the extent that Lean challenges the established professional hierarchy and is perceived as diminishing the autonomy of health professionals, it is likely to engender resistance.

It is also at this point that Lean begins to attract more widespread attention from the media and the opposition. As organizations like SUN begin to make their concerns public, the media start to ask increasingly pointed questions about Lean's goals and its achievements. By the spring of 2014, Lean's implementation was subjected to a barrage of media, public and health sector criticism. There is ridicule over reports of bureaucrats and health professionals being required to use Japanese terminology like *hoshins* and *kaizens* instead of "priority" or "continuous improvement". More seriously, the government's insistence that Lean was saving the system money was met with accusations that it was not really about quality improvement but rather about cost-cutting. SUN linked Lean to decreases in patient safety.[83,84,85] A government survey of health care workers found 64% of doctors questioned Lean techniques and goals.[86]

In the legislative assembly, the opposition NDP attacked the government for what it characterized as the excessive spending involved in the C$40M consultant's contract, including bringing in *Senseis* from Japan to lead Lean workshops for health system managers across the province.[87,88]

The Saskatchewan government seemed unprepared for the criticism. Though the government insisted that Lean has resulted in significant cost-savings and improvements in care,[89] there is little independent evidence that such is the case. The government did, however, eventually cancel the contract with Black and Associates, declaring that provincial officials were now sufficiently trained to carry on Lean implementation themselves.[90]

This was simultaneously an implementation and a communications failure on the part of the government. It never fully grasped the difficulty of implementing Lean in an environment characterized by multiple centers of decision-making authority and stakeholders with professional and regulatory autonomy. It was the government that went ahead with the rolling out of a policy innovation that it had to know would be disruptive to the status quo inside the health care system and yet it made little effort to ensure the cooperation of those who had the capacity, for good reasons or bad, to derail the implementation.

On the communications side, the government soon lost the public relations war over Lean. It stuck almost exclusively to the defense that whatever had been spent on Lean implementation, was more than made up for by what was saved in efficiencies. But this only increased suspicion that Lean was about cuts and cost-saving and not really about "patient- centeredness" and "empowered workers". The government has yet to offer any substantive indication that quality of care has improved as a direct result of Lean's implementation.

When Lean was described as a cult and its curious language likened to Scientology, it mattered little in the public's mind whether it was saving much money or not.

[End reproduced article]

Reprinted with permission via Creative Commons License. © (2016). Health Reform Observer.

Analysis of Saskatchewan Lean Challenges

Undertaking one of the largest Lean transformations in healthcare meant that there were a number of things that could go wrong. However, regardless of the size or scale of transformation, there are some key takeaways that other organizations can learn from to avoid making the same mistakes. In this case, leadership—the government—didn't foresee a significant difference between back-office operations and full-scale health system transformation. Therefore, the Lean system wasn't adapted in a pilot prior to a full-scale implementation.

Lack of piloting, ongoing communication issues, and a change in the status quo led to additional challenges. The Lean transformation approach challenged the professional hierarchy, which diminished the autonomy of health professionals both in perception and reality. The leadership behind the Lean transformation knowingly disrupted the status quo with little effort to ensure cooperation of key stakeholders who could potentially derail the implementation.

Though cost savings were touted, there was little real and hard evidence. Thus, either there was actually a lack of cost savings or a neglect by the consultant and government to adequately track the cost advantages. With a $40 million contract, citizens and the workforce expect hard financial and/or clinical gains to outweigh the cost. Without such evidence, the value of Lean and the consulting contract were clearly in question. McIntosh dives into more detail with strengths, weaknesses, opportunities, and threats of the failed/stalled implementation in Table 8, originally published in the same article previously cited.

Table 8: SWOT Analysis of Lean in Saskatchewan (reprinted from article)

Strengths	Weaknesses
• Committed leadership and policy champions inside Saskatchewan Health • Committed political leadership from Minister and Premier • Some evidence of gains made through initial implementation • Willingness to invest in implementation and wide-scale training	• Failed to properly evaluate initial implementation • Failed to account for autonomy of key professions in decision to scale up • Processes for empowering patients never had clear public buy-in. • Rigid insistence on adoption of new language and concepts made it look like a "top-down" process.
Opportunities	Threats
• First jurisdiction to attempt such a wide-scale application of Lean processes • Could provide significant voice for patients in managing their own care • Possibility of measurable quality improvement and some cost-saving	• Unions and professional associations had different political and policy agendas and the autonomy to pursue them • Media quickly focused on issues that made government look rigid, silly or incompetent • Public and media concern over cost of consultants and unnecessary spending

Mitigating Weaknesses and Threats

Learning from Lean challenges in Saskatchewan, both threats and weaknesses shown in Table 8, organizations can mitigate challenges proactively.

Lean practitioners must respect both where the organization is and from where it has come. Learning from past mistakes and past success with other initiatives will give insight into how to best to mitigate challenges to Lean transformation. Exploring potential failure modes, before transformation starts or is scaled-up, even when success seems obvious, is critical to mitigating challenges.

In any transformation, accounting for the autonomy of key professionals is of the upmost importance. As discussed in Chapter 3, using Lean as only a process improvement methodology can have unintended consequences, which may be exacerbated when physicians, unionized workforce, or autonomous professionals experience first- or second-hand negative impacts of Lean transformation. Those professionals must have a hand in developing the approach, thereby owning and improving upon the pitfalls.

Additionally, when unions and professional associations have different political and policy agendas, social compacts can be used to find and stick to common ground, especially when the associations also have the autonomy to pursue different agendas. Compacts, defined in the first article by Kaplan et al., are "reciprocal agreements between the institution and physicians, leaders, board members [unions and other autonomous associations] defining the responsibilities and expectations for all parties."

Also stated in the first article by Kapan, et al, a common transformation language is necessary, but that doesn't mean an improvement language didn't exist before the introduction of Lean terminology at an organization. Rather than bringing the token Lean-language infused with Japanese and manufacturing terms, learn and adopt the current improvement language of both the organization and industry. This makes for a more holistic transformation process, rather than a perceived top-down rigid process.

Having a perceived top-down rigid process causes those impacted to be particularly critical, especially when tax-payers or owners are paying for the transformation. As in the case of Saskatchewan, the media and public focused on unnecessary spending and issues that made the government look incompetent. Challenges like these are reasons to start small before scaling up quickly, celebrate successes, and track financial gains to demonstrate the cost-benefit of Lean. Don't scale up immediately and spend an exorbitant amount of money, like Saskatchewan did to the tune of $40 million dollars.

Start small, think big, grow resources internally from the elimination of waste.

Rolling Out Lean Production Systems

The next article primarily deals with manufacturing but can be used to better understand successes and failures of Lean roll-outs in many industries. The authors of *Rolling Out Lean Production Systems* argue that the effectiveness and efficiency of Lean roll-outs is higher when:

- Lean knowledge codification (specificity of administering the knowledge) is lower;

- autonomy of the plant is higher;

- leaders can align the organization and adapt Lean thinking simultaneously.

Essentially this means that Lean roll-outs should be based on principles, autonomy, and contextual ambidexterity, which are all explained during and after the article. After the article, I provide concrete examples of challenges at the end of the chapter.

Article 4: "Rolling Out Lean Production Systems: A Knowledge-Based Perspective."
R. Secchi & A. Camuffo

Knowledge replication strategy and lean roll-out performance

As reported in the literature on the replication of organizational knowledge, there is no unanimous consensus on the direction and intensity of the effect of template-based vs principle-based approaches on lean roll-out performance. Our case studies show that a principles-based roll-out process creates the conditions for a self-directed learning process in the plant, characterized by a more active approach to experimentation and self-discovery, which is the ultimate meaning of lean thinking.[91] This approach led the relevant plants to better understand how to apply a lean logic to their contexts, to grasp possible problems and foresee solutions, ending up with a faster and more satisfying roll-out.

This evidence is in some ways consistent with the most recent research on the nature of lean systems.[92] Complexity requires a conceptualization that goes beyond the idea of a system of practices[93,94] to promote the idea of a management system that includes organizational routines, learning routines, organizational culture and leadership. Contrary to conventional wisdom, which suggests that the more codified the knowledge to be transferred is, the easier and better the transfer process, we argue that some level of ambiguity is functional to enable and trigger local learning and adaptation processes. This conceptualization is consistent with studies that theorize lean systems as a dynamic capability or an organizational capability to systematically question, renovate and improve its routines, remaining engaged in unceasing loops of organizational learning.[95,96] This approach to knowledge generation and change applied to lean roll-out processes postulates room for experimentation, trials and errors[97,98] and sees the diffusion of lean operations practices as a knowledge creation process of operational processes and how to change them.[99] Based on our evidence and this conceptualization of the lean system as complex, causally ambiguous and more oriented to a dynamic approach to learning and knowledge creation rather than to simple replication, we argue that lean roll-out processes are likely to be more effective and efficient when they are principles-driven rather than template-driven. To formulate our proposition, we conceive a principles-driven roll-out as a process with a lower degree of codification of the knowledge associated with the lean operations practices to be disseminated and the process itself:

P1. The lower the degree of lean knowledge codification, the higher the effectiveness and efficiency of the lean roll-out process.

Decision-making decentralization and lean roll-out performance

In the theory section [located in the original article], we show that there is generally some evidence that decision-making centralization operates as a facilitator of within-organization knowledge transfer activities, especially between the parent company and plants in

MNCs [multi-national companies]. Indeed, direct involvement and control from HQ [headquarters] has proven to be an effective strategy for successful HQ-plant knowledge transfer. However, another substantial body of empirical evidence suggests that knowledge transfer processes that are closely driven and controlled by HQ reduce the level of engagement of the plants and frustrate the plant management team's propensity to make consistent and coordinated use of local resources to facilitate the lean roll-out process.

The anecdotal evidence emerging from the multiple case analysis suggests that the benefits of decentralization and plant autonomy in the lean roll-out process more than offset the supposed advantages of tighter HQ control in knowledge transfer performance. Decentralization not only facilitates local adaptation but also obliges the plant to not adopt the lean operations practices as a "foreign body" of "things to do on top of the rest" but to make sense of them and their implementations in light of the plant's strategic goals, objectives, problems and priorities.

A more decentralized approach to lean roll-outs is also consistent with the organizational approach and management philosophy underlying lean thinking. Most lean literature (both scholarly and practitioner oriented) underlines that lean management systems constitute a dynamic capability. This is basically rooted in multiple-level, collective problem-solving, tapping into people ingenuity at all levels and management behaviors geared towards supporting rather than directing others' behaviors, stimulating self-discovery, exploring new knowledge and continuous learning.[100,101] Overall, the evidence emerging from our case studies and the comparative performance of the lean roll-outs lead us to argue that decentralization, in the form of greater plant management autonomy, is beneficial to the success of the lean roll-out process. Thus, we formulate the following proposition:

P2. The higher the degree of autonomy of the plant, the higher the effectiveness and efficiency of the lean roll-out process.

Prevalent type of ambidexterity and lean roll-out performance

As illustrated in the theory section [again, located in the original article], lean roll-outs can be conceptualized as processes that entail at least some level of ambidexterity. Plants involved in lean roll-out processes engage in exploration, innovation and change processes (the introduction of new lean operations practices, often unknown and never experimented) while at the same time performing daily operations to achieve the current objectives.[102] In the cases analyzed, plant management teams simultaneously pursued the exploitation of existing operational capabilities and the exploration of new operational capabilities. An ambidextrous plant-level organization is a key enabler of lean roll-outs and our case studies, consistently with the outstanding literature, suggest that this goal can be achieved in two different ways, either through structural or contextual ambidexterity.

Although in all the cases analyzed some type of duality in the organizational structure at the plant level emerged (either through massive but temporary intervention of the HQ LPO or through the constitution of a permanent local team of lean specialists), the most efficient and effective roll-outs seem to be characterized by a more contextual approach. Contextually ambidextrous plant organizations seem to enable a better introduction of lean operations practices, a percolation process that although posing the challenge all the way down to the employee level to integrate explorative and exploitative activities, connects the new routines directly to the plant management problems, objectives and priorities and embeds them in individual and collective behaviors.

A more contextual approach seems to generate more opportunities for proactive cognition and behavior[103] such as increased energy and self-efficacy[104] at the plant level.

Our cross-case analysis shows that the comparatively more effective and efficient lean roll-out processes are associated with plant organizations in which, via contextual ambidexterity, there is more room for diffused experimentation and unplanned learning with regard to the introduction of lean operations practices.

In such environments, lean knowledge is engendered and enacted by the everyday actions of plant managers and employees, rather than through top-down, HQ or lean specialist-driven knowledge transfer. Contextual ambidexterity renders lean roll-out a plant learning process that occurs not in parallel but is integrated with ongoing activities. This view of lean roll-outs as open ended, discovery and learning processes[105] and the correlated need to adopt a more contextual approach in the organization of the knowledge transfer process at the plant level is also aligned with the lean thinking philosophy and with the conceptualization of lean systems as dynamic capabilities.[106,107] Hence, our third proposition:

P3. The more the lean roll-out process is based on contextual ambidexterity, the higher the effectiveness and efficiency of the lean roll-out process.

[End of excerpt]

Reprinted with permission from Emerald Group Publishing Limited, originally published in *International Journal of Operations & Production Management*, 36, no. 1 © Emerald Group Publishing Limited 2016.

Challenges with Extending Lean Transformation

The authors essentially suggest that rolling-out Lean systems results in unnecessary challenges or even failure when there is:

1. high Lean knowledge codification, meaning the roll-out is more template-driven than principles-driven, which I'll refer to as the *template over principles* challenge;

2. lower autonomy of the facility, or *centralized challenge*, meaning that the roll-out is centralized and corporate-based rather than decentralized and local;

3. structural ambidexterity, or *structural over context challenge*, meaning there is more emphasis on structure than context of

Lean. (Ambidexterity refers to the organization being able to transform for the future while simultaneously continuing to conduct business.)[108]

Template-Driven Challenge. Lean may fail if there is a high degree of knowledge codification, meaning that Lean is template-driven as opposed to principles-driven. This essentially means that the organization emphasizes the templates used in a Lean transformation over and above the principles behind them.

Templates might include problem-solving sheets, specific metric reports, A3s, specific improvement forms, project charters, workplace organization audits, kanban cards, andon boards, and other specific and well-defined Lean tools and templates. Table 9 below shows different examples along with the potential impact on failure by taking a template-driven approach.

Table 9: Examples of Template- vs. Principles-driven Impact on Lean Failure

Lean Concept: Problem-Solving. Principles Versus Template Examples and Challenges	
Template	From the leader: "Fill out this A3, using these specific boxes, and you'll be able to solve the problem better!"
Challenge	From the learner: "Why am I wasting my time just filling out these sections on a form?"
Overcoming the Challenge	A better approach from the leader: "How can we keep this problem from happening again? Let's write it down, execute, and follow up."
Lean Concept: Hoshin-Kanri (annual planning). Principles Versus Template Examples and Challenges.	
Template	From the leader: "Create an X-Matrix (visual tool for annual planning) and we will have a great cascaded plan for everyone to see!"
Challenge	From the learner: "Why do I have to fill out this complicated template when I can just start to improve results?"
Overcoming the Challenge	A better approach from the leader: "How can we best visualize and check the plan on a regular basis to achieve our goals?"

Lean Concept: Improvement / Suggestion System. Principles Versus Template Examples and Challenges.	
Template	From the leader: "Fill out the form if you want your $10 gift card for making an improvement!"
Challenge	From the learner: "I want to make improvements and be recognized, but I have to fill out this silly form first!"
Overcoming the Challenge	A better approach from the leader: "What improvements did your team make today? Let's go thank those folks!"
Lean Concept: Value Stream Mapping. Principles Versus Template Examples and Challenges.	
Template	From the leader: "Use these symbols for value, waste, kaizen, to show your improvement! Make sure you put it all on an A3!"
Challenge	From the learner: "Why do I have to calculate non-value-added time when we can't even agree on the right sequence of steps?"
Overcoming the Challenge	A better approach from the leader: "Let's visualize process where necessary; what are the actions to improve?" Check. Adjust.

Centralized Challenges

Centralized challenge occurs when the facility has lower autonomy, so the roll-out is centralized and corporate rather than decentralized and local. If the facility is not sufficiently empowered to solve its own problems and develop its own framework for problem solving, it may be "checking a box" on a Lean toolkit rather than adapting and creating a learning system to make and sustain change.

Note that localizing a Lean roll-out process does not mean that the facility is left on its own to just figure it out. The headquarters still needs to support, like sending a coach or sensei, and to provide knowledge via the knowledge-sharing processes discussed in the previous chapter. Table 10 demonstrates examples of centralized and decentralized elements and challenges.

Table 10: Impact of Local and Corporate Roll-outs on Lean Failure

Decentralized (Local)	Centralized (Corporate)	**Lean Transformation Challenges**
Allowing the facility to choose processes to measure that impact the corporate goals.	Mandating which processes are measured to achieve corporate goals.	Facilities not selecting and analyzing problems themselves. Facilities focusing on the wrong process indicators and not making progress toward the corporate goals.
Establishing Lean daily management guidelines for improvement.	Establishing very specific corporate standards for Lean daily management.	Following a strict protocol of tools without focusing on results.
Best practices designed at the local level and shared.	Standards designed by upper management and pushed down on the organization.	Facilities not owning, sustaining, and improving upon the corporate standards.

Structural Challenges

Ambidexterity means the ability to use both the right and left hand with equal skill.[109] In terms of transformation, it means that the organization is able to transform for the future while simultaneously continuing to conduct business, which results in the organization aligning and adapting simultaneously.

If the organization and its leaders view transformation and everyday work as separate, this is defined as the "And Lean" or "And Operational Excellence" problem. Meaning that the organization and its leaders have to continue to do business as usual "and" Lean. Lean concepts are viewed as additions and not as integrated into daily activities to achieve results. The goal is to be able to do Lean both contextually and structurally.

Examples in Table 11 provide context for both structural and contextual ambidexterity for challenges in Lean transformation.[110] Structural, for example, includes using kaizen teams or master black belts for projects. Contextual, for example, is teaching everyone to solve problems and having internalized systems for front line workers to create improvements. Emphasizing structural over contextual may lead to a lack of cultural change and the learning necessary for transformation.

Table 11: Structural and Contextual Ambidexterity's Impact on Lean Failure[111]

	Structural	**Contextual**	**Lean Transformation Challenges**
Achieved by	Separate unit/ teams	Exploration by individual employees	Using kaizen teams to establish new standards versus creating the culture for individuals to explore improvement.
How senior leadership guides behavior	Define the structure	Develop the context	Overemphasis on quickly making the numbers versus creating a learning organization to sustainably make (and keep) the numbers.
Workforce Lean skills	Specialists	Generalists	Having, for example, Lean teams, six sigma black belts, or other specialists solve problems versus everyone learning how to solve problems.
Transformation led by	CEO and senior leadership	Lean Steering Committee	Having a Lean Steering Committee structurally different than senior leadership creates a dual organizational structure instead of integrating expectations into the authority structure.[112]
Meetings	Improvement integrated into operational meetings	Separate meeting to discuss Lean initiatives.	Separating operations from improvement, instead of improving operations through every day activities.

Conclusion

There are a number of lessons to learn from one of the largest Lean transformations in healthcare. Leadership must foresee a significant difference between back-office operations, small-scale implementation, and full-scale health system transformation. A Lean system must be adapted in a pilot prior to a full-scale implementation. Lean transformation will challenge the professional hierarchy and status quo and must be actively managed and continually communicated. Hard cost savings and improved earnings attributed to transformation must be tracked and communicated to the appropriate audience.

Lean roll-out will have a higher degree of success if it is principles-driven, the facility is autonomous, and it emphasizes contextual ambidexterity. Leaders should focus on a principles-driven roll-out so that others in the organization, especially middle management, can focus on the context of transformation in everyday work. Additionally, adaptation is needed during the roll-out process, as corporate-driven and template-driven emphasis will likely lead to failure.

Table 12: Things to Consider When Extending Lean

When Extending Lean Don't . . .	When Extending Lean Do . . .
Have a separate steering committee for transformation.	Integrate the planning and architecture senior leaders.
Just create a team of specialists to solve problems.	Create a team of coaches to support senior leaders.
Establish a top-down, template-driven approach.	Create a local approach based on top-driven context.
Name the transformation to create hype.	Communicate *"why"* and *"how"* to the workforce on an ongoing basis.
Hire a permanent VP that is ultimately responsible for transformation.	Hire a temporary (for a few years) expert that can coach the CEO.
Create a dual organization structure (Lean Steering Committee)	Integrate Lean transformation into senior leaders' work.

CHAPTER 5

Sustaining Transformation

Sustaining Transformation is the final and most difficult step on the Lean journey, because it is essentially never-ending. Very few organizations have ever been considered "Lean" over the past few decades, and even fewer of them actually remain that way. This chapter primarily focuses on the transformation and eventual failure of Saturn as well as highlights from Wiremold at the end of the chapter.

I chose to discuss the Saturn story because Saturn was widely successful, emulated Toyota, and the resources and people involved were immense. Just the same, the disappointment after the Saturn brand ended is still felt by Saturn lovers today. This chapter is based on Joe Sherman's book *In the Rings of Saturn.*[113] Other businesses, unfortunately, have a very similar ending to their Lean transformations as Saturn's, and many of today's Lean success stories will end the same if past mistakes in Lean transformation are not understood.

Saturn Becoming Lean

In 1985, facing shrinking profits and market share, automobile giant General Motors needed to reestablish both its power and influence within the automotive market. GM embarked on the largest one-time investment in the history of the United States at the time: a $5 billion initiative to compete with Japanese and other automobile imports, creating 6,000 jobs directly plus an estimated 15,000 more indirectly. By April 1992, GM's new subsidiary, Saturn, had been awarded the highest rating for mechanical reliability by *Consumer Reports*, and J.D. Powers ranked Saturn third in customer satisfaction, behind only luxury nameplates Lexus and Infinity. Despite the initial success, however, rising to the top and remaining there provided to be a challenge as the Saturn experiment progressed.

General Motors hoped to learn from past mistakes and current opportunities, including experiences at its Vega and Freemont plants. In 1972, for example, GM management chose tough disciplinary action at the Vega plant to deal with high absenteeism, production slowdowns, and perceived product sabotage. The United Auto Workers (UAW) fought back with claims of poor working conditions, "boot camp" style disciplinary action, and defective and poor-quality cars caused by prioritizing productivity above quality. Neither GM nor the UAW worked to solve the real problem: a lack of mutual trust and respect.

Learning from the Pilot

Roger Smith, CEO of General Motors from 1981 to 1990, understood that he couldn't directly compete with the Japanese, so he endorsed and pushed through a plan to partner with Toyota. One objective was for GM managers to witness how the Japanese operated with high quality, low costs, and high productivity. In addition, Smith wanted GM management to learn how the company's labor and management got along so well.

At the Fremont plant, GM began to learn from the lessons of New United Motor Manufacturing, Inc. (NUMMI), GM's joint venture with Toyota. For Toyota, the main purposes of the alliance were rapid entry to the US market and learning to work with an American workforce.[114] The purpose for General Motors was to learn the Toyota Production System first hand and to produce a small car.[115] This 1983 joint venture proved initially successful for both Toyota and General Motors.

Rolling-Out Lean

In the same year that GM was learning from Toyota at NUMMI, GM formed the "Group of 99" to eventually push what became Saturn to a new level of General Motors operations. This group was chosen from 55 GM plants in 17 divisions and included UAW workers and GM plant managers. The mission statement of the study was: "To identify and recommend the best approaches to integrate people and technology to competitively manufacture small cars in the United States."[116] Essentially, the Group of 99 set out to answer the question: "If we were to start a new car company from scratch, how would we do it?"

The Group of 99 was embarking on a completely new journey that had never been undertaken before within General Motors, nor in most—if any—other car companies. So, the group attended seminars and went to Japanese car manufacturers like Toyota, as well as their suppliers and dealers. They visited companies such as Volvo, Hewlett-Packard, and others. They also spoke with academics to learn the latest, best theories and practices.

Transformation Over Emulation

Many other American companies were shifting to "emulation mode" at the time, meaning that they were attempting to copy the Japanese in an effort to compete. However, Saturn stood apart from the rest of GM. It accepted the need for "integrated business systems" and "enlightened people relationships."[117]

Given GM's history and Saturn's goals, the labor-management relationship had to be tackled first. Due to the decades of conflict between General Motors and its employees, it was extremely difficult for labor and management to create openness, mutual trust, and respect. Teamwork, mutual trust/respect, and shared decision making remained the goals of Saturn.

The Saturn People Philosophy Summary Statement was intended to reflect GM's desire that cooperation be put at the forefront at Saturn, and was also part of the labor agreement there: "We believe that all people want to be involved in decisions that affect them, care about their jobs and each other, take pride in themselves and in their contributions and want to share in the success of their efforts."[118] To operationalize that statement, pay and incentive packages for Saturnites included hiring for life, lower wages compared to other GM factories, and bonuses based on production.

Saturn desired an enlightened workforce that operated bottom up, where decisions were made at the lowest level possible and by consensus. One individual defined his role at the onset of Saturn as: thinking, learning, hiring, grasping quality, laying out his own work area, linking his area to the next steps adjacent to his, developing an individual training plan, and participating in meetings about leadership, safety, and quality.

From a leadership standpoint, there were three clearly defined layers, each with distinct powers. At the team level, teams were self-directed, meaning that they ran their own shows and were responsible for a number of things for which teams were traditionally not responsible: housekeeping, inventory control, and producing to schedule. Self-direction also meant in part that they initiated and implemented actions via consensus.

Team-level responsibilities at Saturn:[119]

- Run its own show
- Inventory control
- Hold meetings
- Produce to schedule
- Conduct repairs
- Keep good records
- Create quality product
- Undertake scrap control
- Make improvements continually
- Perform to budget
- Control absenteeism
- Act in a self-directed manner, initiating action from consensus
- Take care of housekeeping
- Communicate and cooperate with adjacent teams
- Operate and maintain the line
- Stay flexible to get the line up and running

The employee performance, consultation, and discipline system also was very clear. Previously, it may have taken two years for an individual to be fired from the General Motors, while the UAW and management battled. Now, with two clear zones for consultation/discipline (amber and red zones), whether the issue was attendance or other disciplinary matters, the final warning resulted in a three-day suspension with pay so the employee could consider whether or not he or she wanted to work for Saturn. Though some people were fired due to the policy, life-long employment was an opportunity for everyone. Cooperation between management and the union reduced the time needed to terminate a worker from two years to six months.

At Saturn's peak, it emulated Toyota—in particular, it paralleled the NUMMI plant. This put General Motors in a position to compete with the Japanese directly from both a product and Lean philosophy standpoint. Saturn's goal was people-centric, achieving a unity of purpose and teamwork. However, the Saturn culture clashed with that of the rest of General Motors, which led to its downfall.

Challenges to Sustaining Transformation

At around the same time that Saturn was being recognized by J.D. Powers and Consumer Reports, the company began spinning out of orbit, so to speak. The following explores many different causes of Saturn's difficulties, leading to the eventual end of production in 2009. Figure 3 shows these causes in a fishbone diagram, divided into four categories: The Saturn Business, GM Culture & Leadership, Compensation, and Structure.

The Saturn Business

Though Saturn was a relatively new company and brand, it was not the only American-made small car competing with the likes of Toyota. Near Saturn's end, General Motors was losing billions and close to bankruptcy. Due to a number of issues—such as the demand to produce more cars, extended hours, and weekend work—as well as production problems, Saturn had difficulty maintaining a quality car.[120] As competition increased and car quality was not maintained, it became difficult for Saturn to sustain positive brand awareness and profitability.[121] Saturn's profits were weak due to a combination of strong competition, low margins, and production volumes below projections.[122]

One of the reasons for missed production was mis-management of kanban and just-in-time inventory—extremely difficult concepts to fully integrate. Some areas of the plant stockpiled parts while other areas worked overtime, unable to keep up with production. The kanban system lacked *keiretsu*, the interlinking network of suppliers and manufacturers that supports the system. In some cases, inefficiencies in the kanban system brought production to a halt, thereby reducing overall output.

This decline in the Saturn business, along with management system changes from GM and the United Auto Workers (UAW), put Saturn leadership in a catch-22. If management continued to empower teams to do a good job, team members might become redundant. Thus, management might be forced to lay off the same team members who created the improvements. Due to pressures from General Motors, Saturn managers knew that the risk of continued empowerment would negatively impact employees' jobs.

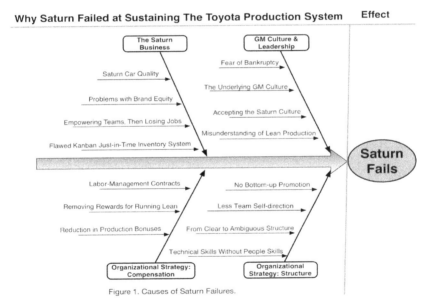

Figure 1. Causes of Saturn Failures.

Figure 2. Fishbone Diagram on Why Saturn Failed

General Motors Culture and Leadership

The chairman of General Motors preached the consolidation of GM plants and linked this to Lean manufacturing. He emphasized that Lean was the future of General Motors. Joe Sherman, who experienced the zeal of the workers' team approach using Lean, wondered if the chairman even "knew what he was talking about" when he described Lean.[123]

Saturn was a completely different culture from that of the rest of General Motors, so it was extremely difficult to transfer the Saturn culture to the rest of GM, including its leadership. Past GM and UAW clashes meant that many individuals brought with them to Saturn that same clashing culture. Every prospective employee had an underlying sense of the General Motors culture, labor rules, and union grievances, and in some cases, an indifference toward the success of GM but a militant mindset for the labor rules. Accepting the Saturn culture was difficult. As things started to shift at Saturn, some employees wanted to revert to the old GM ways.

Transferring the Saturn style of labor meant everything would have to change at General Motors from a human relations standpoint. But a confrontational style was engrained into the culture at General Motors.[124] In fact, neither GM upper management nor the United Auto Workers International welcomed the Saturn culture. Because GM leadership culture did not mesh with that of Saturn, the Saturn culture did not spread, and the old GM culture eventually took over.

Compensation

The production bonus provision of the labor contract was slashed from 20% to 5%[125] while wages went up. This put Saturn in a precarious position where base compensation was more fixed and not tied to production: Workers made nearly the same amount regardless of output. Wages would not flex with production as they had in the past, thereby increasing the cost to keep the plant staffed yet not completely productive. It also reduced incentives for workers to achieve production goals.

In the past, teams had been rewarded for running lean, but that changed. Essentially, if a team had 10 people running an operation, but could run the same operation with seven, there was no incentive for reallocating the three people not needed. Profit-sharing and incentives would make this change benefit both the organization and the team. However, because rewards for running lean were removed, teams would continue to run with too many people. This and the compensation structure ultimately proved not to be good for the Saturn workers nor the Saturn business.

Structure

Originally, there were three layers of management, with certain powers defined at each layer. Over time, however, the organizational structure became very vague, to the point where some individuals didn't know where they fit into the structure. Without a distinct structure, roles and responsibilities also became vague.

Teams shifted from being "self-directed" to "self-managed." Essentially, this shifted Saturn to a more top-down direction for decision-making. Teams accepted more decisions and direction from above but had flexibility in how to carry out the directions. Saturnites saw this as a loss of power.

Saturn stopped promoting from the bottom of the organization like it had done in its initial years. A lack of bottom-up promotions means fewer workers wanting to become multi-functional, which decreases the overall flexibility of the organization. Similarly, one educator noted that the education system within Saturn focused on all the technical skills needed but not the people skills. Without constant coaching and development of people skills, it became difficult to deal with problems, remain flexible, and sustain the improvements already made.

Wiremold's End of Lean

Unfortunately, Saturn Corporation was not the only organization to successfully utilize Lean but later experience failure. Wiremold was a well-documented transformation conducted under the leadership of Art Byrne, author of *The Lean Turn Around*. Art adapted the Toyota Production system as the "prescriptive implementation methodology" to turn around Wiremold.[126]

The problem, though, came about a decade after the initiation of transformation, in the "sustaining" phase. The primary owners of the family business were essentially about to cash out due to age and other family priorities, which put the company in a liquidity bind. They looked for other companies to acquire Wiremold, and eventually selected Legrand for a purchase price 1600% above the company's 1990 share level.[127]

After the buyout, the following problems occurred, most likely caused by Wiremold being inadvertently forced to conform to Legrand and eventually leading to the failure of Lean:

1. Resistance from Legrand bosses, which led to:

    a. rapid turnover in management, potentially from hostility toward Legrand;

    b. lack of Lean knowledge within new executives;

    c. overall reduction of kaizen.

2. Emphasizing batch and queue (producing and pushing many pieces to the next process at once) over a Lean, continuous one-piece flow, which led to:

    a. promoting large batch ordering from customers, further leading to a return of unsold items.

    b. batch purchasing and bargaining with suppliers over price, further leading to outsourcing to low-wage countries;

    c. downsizing of the just-in-time promotion office;

    d. standard-cost software further leading to a focus on headcount over the elimination of waste.

Conclusion

This chapter demonstrates that even organizations that use a vast amount of resources to transform, like Saturn, are not immune to Lean transformation challenges. Similarly, organizations like Wiremold, with the best intentions and Lean systems, can see them completely reversed due to one oversight, in this case about how to sustain Lean thinking in ownership transitions.

An organization that desires transformational Lean thinking must focus on institutional culture, management systems, and new leadership approaches. Additionally, to sustain transformation, the most appropriate organizational strategy, including compensation and structure, must be introduced at the most appropriate time and communicated accordingly.

Table 13: Things to Consider When Sustaining Lean

When sustaining Lean Don't . . .	When sustaining Lean do . . .
Quickly make long-lasting decisions due to poor planning.	Have a long-term business strategy with alternatives.
Give unsustainable financial incentives.	Link financial incentives to the performance of the company, once employees understand how they can impact it.
Make a succession plan that kicks in when a senior leader exits.	Create a succession plan that is put into place on a regular basis, creating a multifunctional leadership team.

Afterword

Why Most Companies Are Failing with Lean

Martial Durin, Managing Director, Kaizen Institute China

I started my Lean (Toyota Production System) experience in May 1985. It was a great opportunity and honor to work with and learn from Dr. Shigeo Shingo for three years. One of the first teaching points I learned from my sensei Shingo was the 30 to 40% and 60 to 70% rule: "No more than 30 to 40% of a successful Toyota Production System transformation comes from the tools while 60 to 70% of the success comes from the people."

This was in 1985, and, 30 years later, as Leuschel points out in the many case studies throughout this book, nothing has changed! More specifically, though, there are many other factors that lead to an unsuccessful Lean Transformation.

This is a nonexclusive list of some root causes I recently discussed that Steve asked me to include in this book.

Lack of Respect for People. People are neither machines nor numbers: they are the only appreciating assets of the company and must be respected highly. A good manager is someone who is able to create an excellent and efficient team. It is paramount to consider employees as the highest potential for innovation in the company. This mutual appreciation cannot exist without a code of respect and trust.

As Leuschel and the cited authors discuss in Chapter 1, Lean transformation must emphasize cultural change, different leadership styles, and a new management system with respect for people at the center.

Poor People Management Skills. People management doesn't mean buying peace or managing with excessive authority. Though many managers have the technical skills, they do not have team management skills. As a result, overall teamwork cannot be achieved at the optimum level. Operational excellence requires cross-functional teamwork where the customers (external and internal) are recognized as the key target to satisfy first.

People management skills are particularly weak at the middle management level. This is not because the managers are poor leaders but because they have never been properly trained in team management. Thus, as Leuschel states, starting with and transforming senior leadership and cascading that learning is paramount to success.

Project Versus Strategy. Lean is not a short-term project but a long-term, endless strategy for companies to leverage growth and earnings. Too often, Lean is mistakenly seen as a cost reduction project for companies. Reducing cost is a consequence of reducing waste in a company, but cost cannot be a primary target of Lean.

In Chapter 2, Leuschel points out that many organizations start Lean as a project—whether to improve a process or to cherry-pick a tool, and many times to cut costs. Lean must be a strategy. As a strategy for the company, the Lean direction and vision must be understood at all levels. Tools like Hoshin Kanri, Policy Deployment, X-Matrix, APP, Catch-ball, and so on do not guarantee success. Only people can make a difference by deploying and *executing* the strategy consistently, measuring progress by setting up a few KPIs and executing the strategy strictly without any deviation.

Training Approach Versus Learning by Doing. Lean Transformation is not as simple as following a recipe and getting trained in that recipe. The same ingredients don't guarantee the same result: what makes one company successful will not guarantee success in another. The only workable approach is using cross-functional teamwork and committing to the Learning by Doing approach. In Chapter 3, Leuschel and Inkpen discuss the importance of establishing ongoing learning systems versus one-time training, which is critical to the success of Lean.

Lack of Standards in the Company at All Levels. My sensei, Dr. Shingo, would always say: "There is no game you can play in the world without rules." Standards are defined as the rules to run a business and a company. Fixing any violations or deviations from standards opens up room for improvement to the company.

Taiichi Ohno, who created the foundations of the Toyota Production System, also always said: "Where there is no standard, there is no kaizen. And if there is no kaizen, the company cannot expect to be successful."

Tools Approach Versus Principles-driven. In Chapter 4, Leuschel discusses the need for principles-driven and context-driven transformation over and above tools and structures, especially when rolling-out Lean systems. People, with the right tools, can pick low-hanging fruit. However, all people in the company must think uniformly based on Lean, and eventually everyone will be driven by the same principles and foundations without compromise. Focusing on tools over principles is a mistake.

Lack of Teamwork. The only one way for a company to survive in the long term is cross-functional teamwork. As defined by Dr. Shingo again: "A process is a sequence of steps and each step has its own process but… the optimum of a process is never equal to the sum of the optimums of each step of the process!" This means that maximizing each step of a process is a mistake if it does not strictly meet the requirements of the customer.

Lack of Measurement. Generally, not establishing crystal-clear measurements leads to disputes and excuses. Everybody seems to be right, but everybody could also be wrong. Some managers prefer this style of management, as it buys peace in the short term. However, it can be a very explosive and damaging management style in the long term. It is definitively not the Lean way.

Lack of Abnormality Management with Quick Response Time for Problem Solving. When standards don't exist, people tend to accept violations or abnormalities too easily in daily life. This cannot be accepted.

Any violation/abnormality must be considered an opportunity for improvement and must be solved as quickly as possible, which is known as "quick response time for problem solving." Unfortunately, this process is very often weak in companies, negatively impacting the motivation of employees to propose new improvement ideas.

The number of employee suggestions and ideas is inversely proportional to the lead time used to solve the issues. Employees are most proactive at the beginning of transformation, but if issues are not managed quickly, they will lose motivation and keep quiet.

Lack of an Efficient Decision-making Process. In a company, both material flow and information flow are well known but unfortunately too often stopped by poor decision flow. All process experts—material, production, etc.—can design great processes, but when a problem arises, they tend to stop the process because the decision maker is not present or because decision making consumes too much time. This is intolerable in a mature Lean organization.

Lack of Overall Leadership or a Bold Lean Leader. A Bold Lean Leader creates unwavering passion and excitement for a Lean transformation that drives cultural transformation across the enterprise, resulting in sustained competitive advantage and increased stakeholder value. Bold Lean Leaders tend to undertake, consciously or unconsciously, a discipline called "deliberate practice" to improve personal performance. Reaching great performance levels is not reserved to a preordained few: it is available to everyone, assuming that the right people are on the right bus and at the right seat. The essence of bold leadership can be described as: vision, passion, effective involvement, deliberate practice, effective teamwork, talent multiplication, boldness, and decisiveness.

Local Improvements Versus Improving the Overall Organization. Although Lean often starts in manufacturing—because it provides value-add, is the biggest asset of the company, and contains the most people—overall vision cannot ignore the big picture, including all supporting and administrative operations. If there is waste in manufacturing that negatively impacts lead time, the same waste will occur in admin operations, also dramatically impacting lead times.

Inappropriate Management of Resistance to Change. After six or 12 months of Lean implementation, all companies face some level of resistance to change, both open and silent. Open resistance to change is always easier to manage because it can be seen, while silent resistance to change is far more difficult to detect. One of the common mistakes made by management is spending too much time and energy on convincing people who are referred to by the acronym "CAVE" (Citizens Against Virtually Everything). Management must focus on early adopters or pioneers by supporting them and recognizing and celebrating their improvements. Even if the number of people resisting change is small, do not underestimate the huge power they have in the organization, because those people are permanently in contact with the workforce and it is easy for them to "manipulate" it.

Fear of Losing Power and Fear of the Unknown. One of the reasons why middle management exhibits more resistance to change is a feeling that a new Lean management style, which needs more teamwork than individual work, would lead to a loss of power for them. The daily life of a supervisor is changed dramatically for the better, although the person may neither understand it nor have been trained for the change. Humans, except those with a pioneering nature, do not like change. It is by its nature disturbing, because it forces people to move from a familiar and secure world to the unknown. This is another reason why clear vision and direction must be provided by management to minimize fear of the new Lean world.

Lack of Recognition of Internal Customer/Supplier Relationships. If the internal customers of a company department cannot be clearly identified, and its primary goal is not to satisfy its internal customers unconditionally, then it is not honoring the Lean way. In many companies pushed by management with an objectives-based approach, primary targets are too often department objective achievements rather than company vision achievements. No matter which department in which an employee works, the primary objective must be to satisfy internal and external customers first, then employees, and finally business partners. This cannot be compromised.

Lack of Consistency and Coherence in Lean Deployment. Lean implementation is a top-down process for at least the first five years. It is managed and driven by management, so during this phase, it is mandatory to guarantee the consistency and the coherency of this deployment throughout all the organization. But Lean won't start to show signs of success until the process starts working bottom up, meaning that people who can see the benefits of Lean begin to propose improvements and implement them. This phase is more critical and must be controlled carefully, because there is a risk of deviating from the roadmap. Again, that is why Leuschel proposes starting with leadership first to ensure this alignment.

Short-Term Benefits Orientation Versus Long-Term Strategy. Lean is not a flavor of the month but a lifelong strategy for leveraging company growth and earnings. Toyota has been applying the same approach consistently for over 60 years and they are still using the same approach. It is definitively not what a general manager of a Chinese company told me: "Oh, Lean, we have done Lean, and we completed the project five years ago."

Compromising Lean Principles. Lean can be customized to some businesses but there is no compromise to be made on key Lean principles. Quite often, companies think they are unique, but key Lean principles are the same and universal across all companies. They can be applied in any business category, such as discrete manufacturing, process industries, services, healthcare, catering, government, and so on. In my career, spanning over 30 years, I even implemented Lean in the French administration of jails. Not compromising key Lean principles is based on the same logic as not accepting abnormalities as the normal way to run a business. If a company starts to accept compromises on key Lean principles, it is certain that the company will fail in terms of successful Lean transformation.

Using Lean Primarily as a Cost Reduction Program. Lean is not a cost reduction program. Some companies are extremely cost driven, and in some cases, only cost-driven companies are willing to use Lean as a cost reduction tool. This is a big mistake, since the sequence of priorities is: safety, quality, delivery, cost, and morale; cost cannot be moved to the front, even if cost is crucial for the company. Cost is not a key driver but a consequence of removing the maximum waste from company processes to make cost reduction easy. If the company makes cost its number one KPI, morale and motivation to improve processes will be negatively impacted. This will result in a predictable failure of Lean transformation.

Lack of a Sense of Urgency. A common reason for failure in companies is a lack of a sense of urgency, which happens for two reasons. The first is an inefficient decision-making flow in the company, resulting in long periods before decisions are made. The second is defaulting to an expert approach to find the best solution.

Companies often never actually implement anything concrete despite spending a lot of time evaluating the best solution. As very often taught by Yoshiki Iwata from Toyota, another sensei of mine: "In Lean, a crude and simple solution is always better than slow and elegant."

Understanding the 5R rule is essential: Responsiveness + Reliability + Rhythm + Responsibility + Relevance. A company must be responsive to market and customer demand; it must have reliable quality and customer service; and production must follow the rhythm of customer demand (i.e. *takt*).

More "Niet" and "Catalog" People than "True" People. My sensei, Dr. Shigeo Shingo, classified managers and engineers into three categories:

1. *Niet* **or** *Nyet*: People whose reply is "No" if the idea is not theirs. (Niet means "No" in Russian.)
2. **Catalog:** People who are only able to find solutions somewhere in a catalog, meaning they are very poor at innovating.
3. **True:** People who add value and innovate. Also refer to the discussion of "a Bold Lean Leader."

Dr. Shingo concluded that the issue in companies is that there are more *Niet* and *Catalog* people than *True* people. The people we need are *True*, but they are a minority, much like value-added operations compared to non-value-added operations.

Conclusion

If you are a Bold Lean Leader, you will drive people in the right direction for a successful and sustainable Lean transformation. It is a deliberate practice and a deliberate choice. You will also recognize ownership of the process and successes of your people, as successful Lean transformation must be the initiative of all your employees rather than that of isolated Lean experts, consultants, or gurus.

Remember the 30% to 40% and 60% to 70% rule by my sensei and friend Shigeo Shingo: no more than 30% to 40% of a successful Lean transformation comes from the tools; 60% to 70% comes from people.

Summary of the Reasons Why Most Companies Fail with Lean

- Lack of respect for people
- Lack of people management
- Using Lean as a project instead of a strategy
- Training approach versus learning by doing
- Lack of standards in the company at all levels
- Tools approach versus principles-driven
- Lack of teamwork
- Lack of measurement
- Lack of abnormality management with quick response time
- Lack of efficient decision process
- Lack of overall leadership or a Bold Lean Leader
- Local improvements versus improving the overall organization
- Managing change inappropriately
- Fear of losing power and fear of the unknown
- Lack of recognition of internal customer/supplier relationships
- Lack of consistency and coherence in Lean deployment
- Short-term benefits-oriented versus long term strategy

- Compromising Lean principles
- Using Lean primarily as a cost reduction program
- Lack of a sense of urgency
- More "Niet" and "Catalog" people than "True" people

Appendix A

Lean Challenge Assessment

The Lean Challenge Assessment in Table 14 contains 50 questions developed based on the failure modes discussed throughout this book. The answers are Strongly Disagree (SD), Disagree (D), Agree (A), and Strongly Agree (SA).

Categories include: Change Management, Desire and Purpose for Change, Leadership Commitment, Organizational Routines, Workforce Development, Labor-Management Relationship, Compensation, Organizational Structure, Problem Solving, and Continuous Improvement System.

Senior leaders, Lean leaders, and others can use this assessment in several ways. First, the assessment can be used in a group setting to identify which items the group disagrees and strongly disagrees with, which indicate barriers for transformation. Second, individuals, like a group of internal Lean leaders, can take the assessment, compare answers and discuss outliers.

The internal Lean team (or similar) must first be able to agree before they take on major barriers to Lean transformation. This assessment will help them identify where they may not see eye to eye and have discussions to understand each other.

Table 14: Lean Challenge Assessment

Change Management	SD	D	A	SA
The strategic plan serves as the organization's guide and compass for both long-term and daily behaviors.				
Our Lean roll-out process is context-based over structure.				

We have a high degree of autonomy of business units during the roll-out process.

There is a focus on establishing systems that encourage individuals to prioritize time.

Management operational activities and Lean roll-out activities are blurred and integrated.

Desire and Purpose for Change	SD	D	A	SA
Lean is NOT used primarily as a cost reduction activity.				
The organization has a strong sense of urgency.				
The organization focuses on long-term strategy over short-term benefits.				
The Lean team's work is primarily principles- driven (as opposed to template- and tools-driven).				
Lean is used for an organizational strategy versus simply running process improvement projects.				

Leadership commitment	SD	D	A	SA
Senior leadership and the board of directors are committed to transformation.				
Senior leaders are catalysts for the transformation.				
Senior leaders are architects of transformation.				
Compacts exist for key leadership groups (e.g., senior leaders, board of directors, unions, leadership, etc.)				
Our organization has a "Bold Lean Leader."				

Organizational Routines	SD	D	A	SA
Leaders' daily routines are transparent and predictable.				
Quality and performance improvement are integrated into daily management.				
Quality problems are reviewed and solved daily using gemba walks and floor management activities.				
We have an effective and efficient decision-making process.				
We have a systematic approach to abnormality management with a quick response time for problem solving.				

Workforce Development	SD	D	A	SA
Our organization has a strong respect for people.				
Our organization emphasizes developing people skills.				
We emphasize a learn-by-doing approach as opposed to a training approach.				
There is a sophisticated and effective knowledge management and knowledge transfer process and system.				
We train workers to perform tasks according to standardized procedures.				

Labor-Management Relationship	SD	D	A	SA
Employees believe they can improve themselves out of their jobs but still have a job.				
There is an underlying culture of mutual trust and respect.				
Labor management contracts are mutually beneficial.				
Labor and management are in a cooperative partnership.				
Labor and management are actively involved, together, in the elimination of waste.				

Compensation	SD	D	A	SA
When the company does better financially, the employee does better financially (and vice versa).				
Incentives are based on production (i.e., delivery of a quality service or product).				
Teams are incentivized to eliminate waste and run with fewer people.				
There are clear standards on how to receive pay/benefit increases.				
Raises are based on skill (acquiring new skills to help the organization), not time at the organization.				

Organizational Structure	SD	D	A	SA
The organizational structure is clear on paper and in practice.				
There are clear standards on how to be promoted.				
Leaders promote other leaders that embody transformation.				

	SD	D	A	SA
There is an active plan for bottom-up promotion.				
Teams are self-directed with clear policies.				
Problem Solving	SD	D	A	SA
There is one problem-solving system used across all groups in the organization.				
The organization empowers workers to stop production when quality is threatened.				
We have a standard approach to recovery when processes/equipment are down (not just calling a supervisor).				
Generally, problems are solved with a simple fix over and above introduction of new technology.				
We have an effective total preventative maintenance system (for equipment and processes).				
Continuous Improvement System	SD	D	A	SA
We have one uniform improvement method, language, and approach.				
We involve the entire organization in seeking continual improvements and eliminating waste.				
The number of kaizen events is not reported to Senior Leadership on an ongoing basis.				
The organization differentiates between major kaizen (sophisticated approval process) and minor kaizen (little to no approval process).				
Improvements are local and focused on specific processes versus strategic and oriented toward overhauling complete systems.				

Bibliography

Aaker, David A. "Building a Brand: The Saturn Story." *California Management Review* 36, no. 2 (1994): 114-33.

Adler, P.S. "The 'Learning Bureaucracy': New United Motor Manufacturing, Inc." In *Research in Organizational Behavior* vol. 15, B.M. Staw and L.L. Cummings, eds. Greenwich, CT: JAI Press, 1993.

Ambrosini, Véronique and Cliff Bowman. "Reducing Causal Ambiguity to Facilitate Strategic Learning." *Management Learning* 36, no. 4 (2005): 493-512, https://doi.org/10.1177/1350507605058142.

Anand, G., P. T. Ward, M.V. Tatikonda, and D. A. Schilling. "Dynamic Capabilities Through Continuous Improvement Infrastructure." *Journal of Operations Management* 27, no. 6 (2009): 444-461.

Azadegan, A., P. C. Patel, A. Zangoueinezhad, and K. Linderman. "The Effect of Environmental Complexity and Environmental Dynamism on Lean Practices." *Journal of Operations Management* 31, no. 4 (2013): 193-212.

Barnas, Kim. *Beyond Heroes: A Lean Management System for Healthcare*. Appleton, WI: ThedaCare Center for Healthcare Value, 2014.

Berwick, Donald M. and Andrew D. Hackbarth. "Eliminating Waste in US Healthcare." *JAMA* 307, no. 14 (2012): 1513-16. doi:10.1001/jama.2012.362.

Black, John and David Miller. *The Toyota Way to Healthcare Excellence: Increase Efficiency and Improve Quality with Lean*. Chicago: Health Administration Press, 2008.

Brown, Mark G., Darcy E. Hitchcock, and Marsha L. Willard, *Why TQM Fails and What to Do About It*. Homewood, IL: Business One Irwin, 1994.

Bush, Roger W. "Reducing Waste in US Health Care Systems," *JAMA* 297, no. 87 (2007): 1-4. doi:10.1001/jama.297.8.871.

Camuffo, A., and A. Comacchio. "Diffusion Patterns of Lean Practices: Lessons from the European Auto Industry." In *Automation in Automotive Industries: Recent Developments*, A. Comacchio, G. Volpato, and A. Camuffo, eds. Berlin: Springer Verlag, 1999: 92-118.

Canadian Press. "John Black, U.S. Consultant Hired to Implement Lean, Hard on Saskatchewan in Book." *Regina Leader Post*, May 12, 2016. https://leaderpost.com/business/john-black-u-s-consultant-hired-to-implement-lean-hard-on-saskatchewan-in-book.

Canadian Press. "Sask. Nurses Say They're Being Intimidated Over Lean Program." *CBC Radio-Canada*, April 15, 2014. http://www.cbc.ca/news/canada/saskatchewan/ sask-nurses-say-they-re-being-intimidated-over-lean-program-1.2610542.

Canadian Press. "Stopwatch Used to Track Nurses, Opposition Says." *CBC Radio-Canada*, March 3, 2015. http://www.cbc.ca/news/canada/saskatchewan/ stopwatch-used-to-track-nurse-movements-opposition-says-1.2980795.

CBC News, "Government of Saskatchewan's Lean Contract Comes to an End." *CBC Radio-Canada*, March 31, 2015. http://www.cbc.ca/news/canada/saskatchewan/ government-of-saskatchewan-s-lean-contract-comes-to-an-end-1.3017218.

CBC News, "Nurses Union Having Second Thoughts About 'Lean' Initiative." *CBC Radio-Canada*, March 18, 2014. http://www.cbc.ca/news/canada/saskatchewan/ nurses-union-having-second-thoughts-about-lean-initiative-1.2577677.

CBC News, "Saskatchewan Party Claims $125M in Savings from Lean Program." *CBC Radio-Canada*, March 2, 2015. http://www.cbc.ca/

news/canada/saskatchewan/ saskatchewan-party-claims-125m-in-savings-from-lean-program-1.2979271.

CBC News, "Spending on 'Japanese sensei' questioned by Sask. NDP." *CBC Radio-Canada,* March 14, 2014. http://www.cbc.ca/news/canada/saskatchewan/ spending-on-japanese-sensei-questioned-by-sask-ndp-1.2572507.

Ching, Joan M., Christina Long, Barbara L. Williams, and C. Craig Blackmore. "Using Lean to Improve Medication Administration Safety: In Search of the 'Perfect Dose'." *The Joint Commission Journal on Quality and Patient Safety* 39, no. 5 (2013): 195-204. https://doi.org/10.1016/S1553-7250(13)39026-6.

Crandall, R. E. and W. E. Crandall. "Three Little Words." *Industrial Engineering* 43, no. 6 (2011): 42–47.

Dahlgaard, J. J. and S. M. P. Dahlgaard-Park. "Integrating Business Excellent and Innovation Management: Developing a Culture for Innovation, Creativity, and Learning." *Total Quality Management* 10, no. 4–5 (1999): 465–472

DiMaggio, Paul D. and Walter W. Powell. "The Iron Cage Revisited: Institutional Isomorphism and Collective Rationality in Organizational Fields." *American Sociological Review* 48, no. 2 (Apr., 1983): 147-160.

Dyer, Jeffrey H. and Kentaro Nobeoka. "Creating and Managing a High-Performance Knowledge-Sharing Network: The Toyota Case." *Strategic Management Journal* 21, no. 3 (2000): 345-367.

Emiliani, Bob, David Stec, Lawrence Grasso, and James Stodder, *Better Thinking, Better Results: Case Study and Analysis of an Enterprise-Wide Lean Transformation.* 2nd ed. Kensington, CT: Center for Lean Business Management, LLC , 2007.

Fiss, P. C. "Building Better Causal Theories: A Fuzzy Set Approach to Typologies in Organization Research." *Academy of Management Journal* 54, no. 2 (2011): 393-420.

French, Janet. "Meet John Black: The Management Guru Behind the $39M Saskatchewan Health Makeover." *Saskatoon StarPhoenix* (January 24, 2014) http://www.pressreader.com/canada/saskatoon-starphoenix/20140124/281479274283393.

Furlan, A., A. Vinelli, and G. Dal Pont. "Complementarity and Lean Manufacturing Bundles: An Empirical Analysis." *International Journal of Operations & Production Management* 31, no. 8 (2011): 835-850.

Gagliardi, Pasquale. "The Creation and Change of Organizational Cultures: A Conceptual Framework." *Organization Studies* 7, no. 2 (1986): 117-134. https://doi.org/10.1177/017084068600700203.

Gibson, C. B., and J. Birkinshaw. "The Antecedents, Consequences, and Mediating Role of Organizational Ambidexterity." *Academy of Management Journal* 47, no. 2 (2004): 209-226.

Groopman, Jerome and Pamela Hartzband. "Thinking About our Thinking as Physicians." *ACP Internist* (October 2011), https://acpinternist.org/archives/2011/10/mindful.htm.

Hartzband, Pamela and Jerome Groopman "Medical Taylorism." *New England Journal of Medicine* (January 14, 2016) 374: 106-108. doi: 10.1056/NEJMp1512402.

Hatch, J.M. and A.L. Cunliffe. *Organization Theory: Modern, Symbolic, and Postmodern Perspectives.* Oxford: Oxford University Press, 2013.

Hines, P., M. Holweg, and N. Rich. "Learning to Evolve: A Review of Contemporary Lean Thinking." *International Journal of Operations & Production Management* 24, no. 10 (2004): 994-1011.

Holweg, M. "The Genealogy of Lean Production." *Journal of Operations Management* 25, no. 2, (2007): 420-437.

Inkpen, Andrew. "Learning Through Alliances: General Motors and NUMMI." *California Management Review* 47 no. 4 (2005): 114-136. doi:10.2307/41166319.

Institute of Medicine. *Crossing the Quality Chasm: A New Health System for the 21st Century.* Washington, DC: The National Academies Press, 2001. https://doi.org/10.17226/10027.

Kaplan, Gary S., Sarah H. Paterson, Joan M. Ching, C. Craig Blackmore. "Why Lean doesn't work for everyone." *BMJ Qual Saf* 23 (2014): 970-73, http://dx.doi.org/10.1136/bmjqs-2014-003248.

Kato, I. and A. Smalley. *Toyota Kaizen Methods: Six Steps to Improvement.* Boca Raton, FL: CRC Press, 2010.

Keenan, Tim, David C. Smith, and Jon Lowell. "The Story Behind GM's Costly J-Car Launch." *WardsAuto.* April 1, 1995. https://www.wardsauto.com/news-analysis/story-behind-gms-costly-j-car-launch.

Kenney, M., and R. Florida. *Beyond Mass Production: The Japanese System and its Transfer to the United States.* New York: Oxford University Press, 1993.

Kohn, Linda T., Janet M. Corrigan, and Molla S. Donaldson, eds. *To Err is Human: Building a Safer Health System.* Washington, DC: National Academies Press, 2000.

Kull, T. J., T. Yan, Z. Liu, and J. G. Wacker. "The Moderation of Lean Manufacturing Effectiveness by Dimensions of National Culture: Testing Practice-culture Congruence Hypotheses." *International Journal of Production Economics* 153 (2014): 1–12.

Leape, L., D. Berwick, C. Clancy, J. Conway, P. Gluck, J. Guest, D. Lawrence, et al. "Transforming Healthcare: A Safety Imperative." *BMJ Quality & Safety* 18 (2009): 424-28.

The Leapfrog Group. "The Leapfrog Group announces top hospitals of the decade." The Leapfrog Group. November 30, 2010. http://www.leapfroggroup.org/news-events/leapfrog-group-announces-top-hospitals-decade.

Letmathe, P., M. Schweitzer, and M. Zielinski. "How to Learn New Tasks: Shop Floor Performance Effects of Knowledge Transfer and Performance Feedback." *Journal of Operations Management* 30, no. 3 (2012): 221-236.

Leuschel, S. *Lean Culture Change: Using a Daily Management System.* Indiana, PA: Align Kaizen Publishing, 2015.

Liker, J. K. *The Toyota Way: 14 Management Principles from the World's Greatest Manufacturer.* New York: McGraw-Hill, 2004.

Liker J. K., and J. K. Fran. *The Toyota Way to Continuous Improvement.* New York: Mc-Graw Hill, 2011.

Lillrank, Paul. "The Transfer of Management Innovations from Japan." *Organization Studies* 16, no. 6 (Nov. 1995): 971-89. https://doi.org/10.1177/017084069501600603.

Mandryk, M. "Lean Process Needs More Than Passion." *Regina Leader,* March 19, 2014. http: //www.pressreader.com/canada/leader-post/20140319/281633893184407/TextView.

Mandryk, M. "Explanation for Lean Costs Ridiculous." *Saskatchewan Union of Nurses,* March 4, 2015. http://sun-nurses.sk.ca/communications/news-events/news/item/ ?n=123.

Marksberry, Philip. "Investigating 'The Way' for Toyota Suppliers: A Quantitative Outlook on Toyota's Replicating Efforts for Supplier Development." *Benchmarking: An International Journal* 19, no. 2 (2012): 277-98. https://doi.org/10.1108/14635771211224572.

Mazzocato, Pamela, Carl Savage, Mats Brommels, Håkan Aronsson, and Johan Thor. "Lean Thinking in Healthcare: A Realist Review of the Literature." *BMJ Quality and Safety* 19 (2010): 376-82.

McConnell, K.J., R.C. Lindrooth, D.R. Wholey, T.M. Maddox, and N. Bloom. "Management practices and the quality of care in cardiac units." *JAMA Internal Med* 173 (2013): 684-92. doi: 10.1001/jamainternmed.2013.3577.

McIntosh T. and Ducie M. "Saskatchewan's Health Reform in the Romanow Era: From Restraint to Restructuring," in *Paradigm Freeze: Why it is so Hard to Reform Health Care in Canada,* eds. H. Lazar, P-G. Forest, J. Lavis, J. Church. Montreal/Kingston: Queen's Policy Studies Series, McGill-Queen's University Press, 2013: 1-25.

Mehta, V. and H. Shah, "Characteristics of a Work Organization from a Lean Perspective." *Engineering Management Journal* 17, no. 2 (2005): 14–20.

Meyer, A. D., A. S. Tsui, and C. R. Hinings. "Configurational Approaches to Organizational Analysis." *Academy of Management Journal* 36, no. 6 (1993): 1175-1195.

Miller, D. "Configurations of Strategy and Structure: A Synthesis." *Strategic Management Journal* 7, no. 3 (1986): 233-249.

Miller, Diane, ed. "Going Lean in Health Care." Institute for Health Care Improvement. 2005. https://www.entnet.org/sites/default/files/GoingLeaninHealthCareWhitePaper-3.pdf.

Monden, Y. *Toyota Production System: An Integrated Approach to Just-in-time.* Norcross, GA: Engineering & Management Press, 1998.

"Not-invented-here-syndrome," *Cambridge Business English Dictionary* (Cambridge: Cambridge University Press, 2018), https://dictionary.cambridge.org/us/dictionary/english/not-invented-here-syndrome.

Ohno, Taiichi. *Toyota Production System: Beyond Large-Scale Production.* New York: Productivity Press, 1998.

Pakdil, Fatma and Karen Moustafa Leonard. "Implementing and Sustaining Lean Processes: The Dilemma of Societal Culture Effects." *International Journal of Production Research* 55, no. 3 (2017): 700-717.

Patel, P. C., S. Terjesen, and D. Li. "Enhancing Effects of Manufacturing Flexibility Through Operational Absorptive Capacity and Operational Ambidexterity." *Journal of Operations Management* 30, no. 3 (2012): 201-220.

Perry, Nick and Carol M. Ostrom. "Hospital Details What Went Wrong: Woman Dies from Toxic Injection." *Seattle Times.* November 25, 2004. http://community.seattletimes.nwsource.com/archive/?date=20041125&slug=deathfolo25m.

Poksinska, B. "The Current State of Lean Implementation in Health

Care: Literature Review." *Quality Management in Health Care* 19, no. 4 (2010): 319-329, http://dx.doi.org/10.1097/QMH.0b013e3181fa07bb.

Ragin, C. C. The Comparative Method: Moving Beyond Qualitative and Quantitative Strategies. Berkeley, CA: University of California Press, 1987.

Rapoza, Joshua and James P. Womack. "Getting Started with Lean." *Lean Enterprise Institute*. July 26, 2018. https://www.lean.org/LeanPost/Posting.cfm?LeanPostId=924.

Rother, M. *Toyota Kata: Managing People for Improvement, Adaptiveness and Superior Results*. New York: McGraw-Hill, 2009.

Samuel, Donna, Pauline Found, and Sharon J. Williams. "How Did the Publication of the Book *The Machine That Changed The World* Change Management Thinking? Exploring 25 Years of Lean Literature", *International Journal of Operations & Production Management* 35, no. 10 (2015): 1386-1407. https://doi.org/10.1108/IJOPM-12-2013-0555.

Schudy, C., and H. Bruch. "Productive Organizational Energy as a Mediator in the Contextual Ambidexterity-performance Relation." *Academy of Management Proceedings* 1 (2010): 1-6.

Secchi, R., & A. Camuffo. "Rolling Out Lean Production Systems: A Knowledge-Based Perspective." *International Journal of Operations & Production Management* 36, no. 1 (2016): 61-85.

Shah, R., and P. T. Ward. "Defining and Developing Measures of Lean Production." *Journal of Operations Management* 25, no. 4 (2007): 785-805.

Sherman, Joe. *In the Rings of Saturn*. New York: Oxford Univ. Press, 1994.

Shook, J. "How to Change a Culture: Lessons from NUMMI." MIT *Sloan Management Review* 51, no. 2 (2010): 42-51.

Shook, John Y. "Malpractice in the New England Journal of Medicine." *Lean Enterprise Institute*. February 23, 2016. https://www.lean.org/

LeanPost/Posting.cfm?LeanPostId=539.

Slater, J. "Sask. NDP Finds Lean Survey Troubling." *CKOM News*, September 10, 2014. http://ckom.com/story/sask-ndp-finds-lean-survey-troubling/416019.

Spear S. and H.K. Bowen. "Decoding the DNA of the Toyota Production System." *Harvard Business Review* 77, no. 5 (1999): 96-106.

Spence, Rick. "Top Misconceptions of the Lean Movement, According to Founder Jim Womack" *Financial Post*. October 24, 2013. https://business.financialpost.com/entrepreneur/top-misconceptions-of-the-lean-movement-according-to-founder-jim-womack.

Staats, B. R., D. J. Brunner, and D. M. Upton. "Lean Principles, Learning, and Knowledge Work: Evidence from a Software Services Provider." *Journal of Operations Management* 29, no. 5 (2011): 376-390.

SUN (Saskatchewan Union of Nurses). "President's Message: March 2014—The Real Story About Lean." March, 2014. http://sun-nurses.sk.ca/index/presidents-message/ march-2014-the-real-story-about-lean.

Taitz, Jonathan M., Thomas H. Lee, and Thomas D. Sequist. "A Framework for Engaging Physicians in Quality and Safety." *BMJ Quality & Safety* 21 (2012): 722-28.

Toussaint, John, Patrick H. Conway, and Stephen M. Shortell. "The Toyota Production System: What Does It Mean, And What Does It Mean For Health Care?," *Health Affairs Blog*. April 6, 2016. doi: 10.1377/hblog20160406.054094

Vasilash, G. "GM's Got Game." Automotive Design and Production. November, 2004. www.autofieldguide.com.

Walshe, Kieran. "Pseudoinnovation: The Development and Spread of Healthcare Quality Improvement Methodologies." *International Journal for Quality in Health Care* 21, no. 3 (2009): 153-9.

Wilms, Wellford W. *Restoring Prosperity: How Workers and Managers are Forging a New Culture of Cooperation*. New York: Times Business,

1996.

Womack, James P. and Daniel T. Jones. *Lean Thinking: Banish Waste and Create Wealth in Your Corporation.* New York: Free Press, 2003.

Womack, J. and D. Jones. "From Lean Production to the Lean Enterprise." *Harvard Business Review* 72, no. 2 (1994): 93–103.

Zaidi, Mohamad Faizal Ahmad and Siti Norezam Othman. "Structural Ambidexterity vs. Contextual Ambidexterity: Preliminary Evidence from Malaysia." Full paper proceeding, MISG-2015. GlobalIlluminators vol. 1, 21-34. http://repo.uum.edu.my/15910/1/MISG-15-135.pdf.

Zollo, M., and S. G. Winter. "Deliberate Learning and the Evolution of Dynamic Capabilities." *Organization Science* 13, no. 3 (2002): 339-351.

Notes

---

[1] Donna Samuel, Pauline Found, and Sharon J. Williams, "How did the publication of the book *The Machine That Changed the World* change management thinking? Exploring 25 years of lean literature," *International Journal of Operations & Production Management* 35, no. 10 (2015): 1386-1407, https://doi.org/10.1108/IJOPM-12-2013-0555.

[2] Kieran Walshe, "Pseudoinnovation: The Development and Spread of Healthcare Quality Improvement Methodologies," *International Journal for Quality in Health Care* 21, no. 3 (2009): 153-59, https://doi.org/10.1093/intqhc/mzp012.

[3] Linda T. Kohn, Janet M. Corrigan, and Molla S. Donaldson, eds. *To Err is Human: Building a Safer Health System* (Washington, DC: National Academies Press, 2000).

[4] Institute of Medicine, *Crossing the Quality Chasm: A New Health System for the 21st Century* (Washington, DC: The National Academies Press, 2001), https://doi.org/10.17226/10027.

[5] Nick Perry and Carol M. Ostrom, "Hospital Details What Went Wrong: Woman Dies from Toxic Injection," *Seattle Times,* November 25, 2004. http://community.seattletimes.nwsource.com/archive/?date=20041125&slug=deathfolo25m.

[6] Taiichi Ohno, *Toyota Production System: Beyond Large-Scale Production*

(New York: Productivity Press, 1998).

7 Donald M. Berwick and Andrew D. Hackbarth, "Eliminating Waste in US healthcare," *JAMA* 307, no. 14 (2012): 1513-16, doi:10.1001/jama.2012.362.

8 Roger W. Bush, "Reducing Waste in US Health Care Systems," *JAMA* 297, no. 87 (2007): 1-4, doi:10.1001/jama.297.8.871.

9 James P. Womack and Daniel T. Jones, *Lean Thinking: Banish Waste and Create Wealth in Your Corporation* (New York: Free Press, 2003).

10 K.J. McConnell, et al., "Management Practices and the Quality of Care in Cardiac Units," *JAMA Internal Med* 173 (2013): 684-92, doi:10.1001/jamainternmed.2013.3577.

11 Joan M. Ching, et al., "Using Lean to Improve Medication Administration Safety: In Search of the 'Perfect Dose'," *The Joint Commission Journal on Quality and Patient Safety* 39, no. 5 (2013): 195-204, https://doi.org/10.1016/S1553-7250(13)39026-6.

12 Pamela Mazzocato, et al., "Lean Thinking in Healthcare: A Realist Review of the Literature," *BMJ Quality and Safety* 19 (2010): 376-82.

13 L. Leape, et al., "Transforming Healthcare: A Safety Imperative," *BMJ Quality & Safety* 18 (2009): 424-28.

14 Jonathan M. Taitz, Thomas H. Lee, and Thomas D. Sequist, "A Framework for Engaging Physicians in Quality and Safety," *BMJ Quality & Safety* 21 (2012): 722-28.

15 "The Leapfrog Group Announces Top Hospitals of the Decade," The Leapfrog Group, November 30, 2010. http://www.leapfroggroup.org/news-events/leapfrog-group-announces-top-hospitals-decade.

16 Jeffrey H. Dyer and Kentaro Nobeoka, "Creating and Managing a High-Performance Knowledge-Sharing Network: The Toyota Case," *Strategic Management Journal* 21, no. 3 (2000): 354.

17 Paul Lillrank, "The Transfer of Management Innovations from

Japan," *Organization Studies* 16, no. 6 (Nov. 1995): 971-89, https://doi.org/10.1177/017084069501600603.

18 Fatma Pakdil and Karen Moustafa Leonard, "Implementing and Sustaining Lean Processes: The Dilemma of Societal Culture Effects," *International Journal of Production Research* 55, no. 3 (2017): 700-717.

19 J. Womack and D. Jones, "From Lean Production to the Lean Enterprise," *Harvard Business Review* 72, no. 2 (1994): 93–103.

20 Y. Monden, *Toyota Production System: An Integrated Approach to Just-in-time* (Norcross, GA: Engineering & Management Press, 1998).

21 J. K. Liker, *The Toyota Way: 14 Management Principles from the World's Greatest Manufacturer* (New York: McGraw-Hill, 2004).

22 V. Mehta, and H. Shah, "Characteristics of a Work Organization from a Lean Perspective," *Engineering Management Journal* 17, no. 2 (2005): 14–20.

23 J. K. Liker and J. K. Fran, *The Toyota Way to Continuous Improvement* (New York: Mc-Graw Hill, 2011).

24 J. J. Dahlgaard and S. M. P. Dahlgaard-Park, "Integrating Business Excellent and Innovation Management: Developing a Culture for Innovation, Creativity, and Learning," *Total Quality Management* 10, no. 4–5 (1999): 465–472.

25 R. E. Crandall and W. E. Crandall, "Three Little Words," *Industrial Engineering* 43, no. 6 (2011): 42–47.

26 Dahlgaard and Dahlgaard-Park.

27 Liker, *The Toyota Way*.

28 Gary S. Kaplan, Sarah H. Paterson, Joan M. Ching, C. Craig Blackmore, "Why Lean Doesn't Work for Everyone," *BMJ Qual Saf* 23 (2014): 970-73, http://dx.doi.org/10.1136/bmjqs-2014-003248.

29 Partially adapted from Mark G. Brown, Darcy E. Hitchcock,

and Marsha L. Willard, *Why TQM Fails and What to Do About It* (Homewood, IL: Business One Irwin, 1994).

Chapter Two

[30] Brown, Hitchcock, and Willard, *Why TQM Fails.*

[31] Jeffrey H. Dyer and Kentaro Nobeoka, "Creating and Managing a High-Performance Knowledge-Sharing Network: The Toyota Case," *Strategic Management Journal* 21, no. 3 (2000): 354.

[32] Steven Leuschel, *Lean Culture Change Using a Daily Management System* (Indiana, PA: Align Kaizen Publishing, 2015).

[33] Ibid.

[34] Dyer and Nobeoka, 345-367.

[35] Ibid.

[36] Ibid.

[37] Tim Keenan, David C. Smith, and Jon Lowell, "The Story Behind GM's Costly J-Car Launch," *WardsAuto,* April 1, 1995. https://www.wardsauto.com/news-analysis/story-behind-gms-costly-j-car-launch.

[38] Ibid.

[39] Joshua Rapoza and James P. Womack, "Getting Started with Lean," *Lean Enterprise Institute,* July 26, 2018, https://www.lean.org/LeanPost/Posting.cfm?LeanPostId=924.

[40] Womack and Jones, *Lean Thinking.*

[41] Rick Spence, "Top Misconceptions of the Lean Movement, According to Founder Jim Womack," *Financial Post,* October 24, 2013, https://business.financialpost.com/entrepreneur/top-misconceptions-of-the-lean-movement-according-to-founder-jim-womack.

[42] Diane Miller, ed., "Going Lean in Health Care," Institute for Health Care Improvement, 2005, https://www.entnet.org/sites/default/files/GoingLeaninHealthCareWhitePaper-3.pdf.

43 Kim Barnas, *Beyond Heroes: A Lean Management System for Healthcare* (Appleton, WI: ThedaCare Center for Healthcare Value, 2014).

44 Leuschel, *Lean Culture Change*.

45 S. Spear and H. K. Bowen, "Decoding the DNA of the Toyota production system," *Harvard Business Review* 77 (1999): 103.

46 I. Kato and A. Smalley, *Toyota Kaizen Methods: Six Steps to Improvement* (Boca Raton, FL: CRC Press, 2010), 12.

47 Dyer and Nobeoka, 354.

48 Phillip Marksberry, "Investigating 'The Way' for Toyota Suppliers: A Quantitative Outlook on Toyota's Replicating Efforts for Supplier Development," *Benchmarking: An International Journal* 19, no. 2 (2012): 277-98, https://doi.org/10.1108/14635771211224572.

49 Ibid.

50 Ibid.

51 Leuschel, *Lean Culture Change*.

52 DiMaggio and Powell, "The Iron Cage Revisited."

53 J.M. Hatch and A.L. Cunliffe, *Organization Theory: Modern, Symbolic, and Postmodern Perspectives* (Oxford: Oxford University Press, 2013).

54 Ibid.

Chapter Three

55 John Y. Shook, "Malpractice in the New England Journal of Medicine," Lean Enterprise Institute. 23 Feb. 2016. https://www.lean.org/LeanPost/Posting.cfm?LeanPostId=539.

56 John Toussaint, Patrick H. Conway, and Stephen M. Shortell, "The Toyota Production System: What Does It Mean, And What Does It Mean For Health Care?," *Health Affairs Blog* (April 6, 2016), doi: 10.1377/hblog20160406.054094.

[57] Pamela Hartzband and Jerome Groopman, "Medical Taylorism," *The New England Journal of Medicine* (January 14, 2016), doi: 10.1056/NEJMp1512402.

[58] Jerome Groopman and Pamela Hartzband, "Thinking About our Thinking as Physicians," *ACP Internist* (October 2011), https://acpinternist.org/archives/2011/10/mindful.htm.

[59] Wellford W. Wilms, *Restoring Prosperity: How Workers and Managers are Forging a New Culture of Cooperation* (New York: Times Business, 1996).

[60] Joe Sherman, *In the Rings of Saturn* (New York: Oxford Univ. Press, 1994).

[61] Andrew Inkpen, "Learning Through Alliances: General Motors and NUMMI," *California Management Review* 47, no. 4 (2005): 114-136.

[62] J. Shook, "How to change a culture: Lessons from NUMMI," *MIT Sloan Management Review* 51, no. 2 (2010): 42-51.

[63] Inkpen, "Learning Through Alliances."

[64] Ibid.

[65] For a discussion of the NUMMI production system, see P.S. Adler, "The 'Learning Bureaucracy': New United Motor Manufacturing, Inc.," in B.M. Staw and L.L. Cummings, eds., *Research in Organizational Behavior,* vol. 15 (Greenwich, CT: JAI Press, 1993), 111-194.

[66] The element of the TPS that GM did not initially understand has been called the DNA. See S. Spear and H.K. Bowen, "Decoding the DNA of the Toyota Production System," *Harvard Business Review* 77, no. 5 (1999): 96-106.

[67] Adapted from Inkpen, "Learning Through Alliances."

[68] Inkpen, "Learning Through Alliances" and Véronique Ambrosini and Cliff Bowman, "Reducing Causal Ambiguity to Facilitate Strategic

Learning," *Management Learning* 36, no. 4 (2005): 493-512, https://doi.org/10.1177/1350507605058142.

[69] Shook, "How to Change."

[70] "Not-invented-here-syndrome," *Cambridge Business English Dictionary* (Cambridge: Cambridge University Press, 2018), https://dictionary.cambridge.org/us/dictionary/english/not-invented-here-syndrome.

[71] Inkpen, "Learning Through Alliances."

[72] Ibid.

Chapter Four

[73] Janet French, "Meet John Black: The Management Guru Behind the $39M Saskatchewan Health Makeover," *Saskatoon StarPhoenix* (January 24, 2014), http://www.pressreader.com/canada/saskatoon-starphoenix/20140124/281479274283393.

[74] Canadian Press, "John Black, U.S. Consultant Hired to Implement Lean, Hard on Saskatchewan in Book," *Regina Leader Post* (May 12, 2016) https://leaderpost.com/business/john-black-u-s-consultant-hired-to-implement-lean-hard-on-saskatchewan-in-book.

[75] French.

[76] John Black and David Miller, *The Toyota Way to Healthcare Excellence: Increase Efficiency and Improve Quality with Lean* (Chicago: Health Administration Press, 2008).

[77] Black and Miller, para. 5380.

[78] M. Mandryk, "Lean Process Needs More Than Passion," *Regina Leader*, March 19, 2014, http: //www.pressreader.com/canada/leader-post/20140319/281633893184407/TextView.

[79] T. McIntosh and Ducie M, "Saskatchewan's Health Reform in the Romanow Era: From Restraint to Restructuring," in *Paradigm Freeze:*

Why it is so Hard to Reform Health Care in Canada, eds. H. Lazar, P-G. Forest, J. Lavis, J. Church (Montreal/Kingston: Queen's Policy Studies Series, McGill-Queen's University Press, 2013): 1-25.

[80] SUN (Saskatchewan Union of Nurses), "President's Message: March 2014—The Real Story About Lean," March, 2014, http://sun-nurses.sk.ca/index/presidents-message/ march-2014-the-real-story-about-lean.

[81] Ibid.

[82] B. Poksinska, "The Current State of Lean Implementation in Health Care: Literature Review," *Quality Management in Health Care* 19, no. 4 (2010): 319-329, http://dx.doi.org/10.1097/QMH.0b013e3181fa07bb.

[83] Canadian Press, "Sask. Nurses Say They're Being Intimidated Over Lean Program," *CBC Radio-Canada,* April 15, 2014, http://www.cbc.ca/news/canada/saskatchewan/ sask-nurses-say-they-re-being-intimidated-over-lean-program-1.2610542.

[84] Canadian Press, "Stopwatch Used to Track Nurses, Opposition Says," *CBC Radio-Canada,* March 3, 2015, http://www.cbc.ca/news/canada/saskatchewan/ stopwatch-used-to-track-nurse-movements-opposition-says-1.2980795.

[85] CBC News, "Nurses Union Having Second Thoughts About 'Lean' Initiative," *CBC Radio-Canada,* March 18, 2014, http://www.cbc.ca/news/canada/saskatchewan/ nurses-union-having-second-thoughts-about-lean-initiative-1.2577677.

[86] J. Slater, "Sask. NDP Finds Lean Survey Troubling," *CKOM News,* September 10, 2014, http://ckom.com/story/sask-ndp-finds-lean-survey-troubling/416019.

[87] CBC News, "Spending on 'Japanese sensei' questioned by Sask. NDP," *CBC Radio-Canada,* March 14, 2014, http://www.cbc.ca/news/canada/saskatchewan/ spending-on-japanese-sensei-questioned-by-sask-ndp-1.2572507.

88   M. Mandryk, "Explanation for Lean Costs Ridiculous," *Saskatchewan Union of Nurses*, March 4, 2015, http://sun-nurses. sk.ca/communications/news-events/news/item/ ?n=123.

89 CBC News, "Saskatchewan Party Claims $125M in Savings From Lean Program," *CBC Radio-Canada*, March 2, 2015, http://www. cbc.ca/news/canada/saskatchewan/ saskatchewan-party-claims-125m-in-savings-from-lean-program-1.2979271.

90 CBC News, "Government of Saskatchewan's Lean Contract Comes to an End," *CBC Radio-Canada*, March 31, 2015, http://www.cbc. ca/news/canada/saskatchewan/ government-of-saskatchewan-s-lean-contract-comes-to-an-end-1.3017218.

91 M. Rother, *Toyota Kata: Managing People for Improvement, Adaptiveness and Superior Results* (New York: McGraw-Hill, 2009).

92 R. Shah, and P. T. Ward, "Defining and Developing Measures of Lean Production," *Journal of Operations Management* 25, no. 4 (2007): 785-805.

93 A. Furlan, A. Vinelli, and G. Dal Pont, "Complementarity and Lean Manufacturing Bundles: An Empirical Analysis," *International Journal of Operations & Production Management* 31, no. 8 (2011): 835-850.

94 A. Azadegan et al., "The Effect of Environmental Complexity and Environmental Dynamism on Lean Practices," *Journal of Operations Management* 31, no. 4 (2013): 193-212.

95 G. Anand, et al., "Dynamic Capabilities Through Continuous Improvement Infrastructure," *Journal of Operations Management* 27, no. 6 (2009): 444-461.

96 P. C. Patel, S. Terjesen, and D. Li, "Enhancing Effects of Manufacturing Flexibility Through Operational Absorptive Capacity and Operational Ambidexterity," *Journal of Operations Management* 30, no. 3 (2012): 201-220.

97 Anand, et al., "Dynamic Capabilities."

98 B. R. Staats, D. J. Brunner, and D. M. Upton, "Lean Principles, Learning, and Knowledge Work: Evidence from a Software Services Provider," *Journal of Operations Management* 29, no. 5 (2011): 376-390.

99 Patel, Terjesen, and Li, "Enhancing Effects."

100 P. Hines, M. Holweg, and N. Rich, "Learning to Evolve: A Review of Contemporary Lean Thinking," *International Journal of Operations & Production Management* 24, no. 10 (2004): 994-1011.

101 M. Holweg, "The Genealogy of Lean Production," *Journal of Operations Management* 25, no. 2, (2007): 420-437.

102 Patel, Terjesen, and Li, "Enhancing Effects."

103 C. B. Gibson, and J. Birkinshaw, "The Antecedents, Consequences, and Mediating Role of Organizational Ambidexterity," *Academy of Management Journal* 47, no. 2 (2004): 209-226.

104 C. Schudy, and H. Bruch, "Productive Organizational Energy as a Mediator in the Contextual Ambidexterity-performance Relation," *Academy of Management Proceedings* 1 (2010): 1-6.

105 P. Letmathe, M. Schweitzer, and M. Zielinski, "How to Learn New Tasks: Shop Floor Performance Effects of Knowledge Transfer and Performance Feedback," *Journal of Operations Management* 30, no. 3 (2012): 221-236.

106 Anand, et al., "Dynamic Capabilities."

107 M. Zollo, and S. G. Winter, "Deliberate Learning and the Evolution of Dynamic Capabilities," *Organization Science* 13, no. 3 (2002): 339-351.

108 Based on the reprinted excerpt from Secchi and Camuffo, "Rolling Out Lean."

109 Mohamad Faizal Ahmad Zaidi and Siti Norezam Othman, "Structural Ambidexterity vs. Contextual Ambidexterity: Preliminary Evidence from Malaysia" (full paper proceeding, GlobalIlluminators, MISG-2015, vol. 1, 21-34), http://repo.uum.edu.my/15910/1/MISG-15-135.pdf.

110 Ibid.

[111] Ibid.

[112] Joe Sherman, *In the Rings of Saturn* (New York: Oxford Univ. Press, 1994).

[113] Andrew C. Inkpen, "Learning through Alliances: General Motors and NUMMI." *California Management Review* 47, no. 4 (2005): 114-36. doi:10.2307/41166319.

[114] Wellford W. Wilms, *Restoring Prosperity: How Workers and Managers are Forging a New Culture of Cooperation* (New York: Times [Business, 1996].

[115] Sherman, *In the Rings of Saturn,* 81.

[116] Ibid., 79.

[117] Ibid., 85.

[118] Ibid., 198, 204.

[119] David A. Aaker, "Building a Brand: The Saturn Story," *California Management Review* 36, no. 2 (1994): 114-33 and Sherman, *In the Rings of Saturn.*

[120] Aaker, "Building a Brand."

[121] Ibid.

[122] Sherman, *In the Rings of Saturn,* 284.

[123] Aaker, "Building a Brand."

[124] Sherman, *In the Rings of Saturn,* 273.

[125] Bob Emiliani, David Stec, Lawrence Grasso, and James Stodder, *Better Thinking, Better Results: Case Study and Analysis of an Enterprise-Wide Lean Transformation,* 2nd ed. (Kensington, CT: Center for Lean Business Management, LLC , 2007), 23.

[126] Ibid.

CPSIA information can be obtained
at www.ICGtesting.com
Printed in the USA
BVHW072159290419
546903BV00001B/2/P